GOD'S ETERNAL PLAN

MICHAEL SCANTLEBURY

Word Alive Press
119 De Baets Street Winnipeg, MB R2J 3R9
www.wordalivepress.ca

WORD ALIVE
—P R E S S—

Cataloguing in Publication information is can be obtained from Library and Archives Canada.

BOOKS BY MICHAEL SCANTLEBURY

Understanding the Dual Aspects of Faith
Understanding the Revelation
Are We Living in the End-Times or Last Days?
Heaven and Earth – A Biblical Understanding
Understanding the Kingdom of God and The Church of Jesus Christ
Eschatology – A Biblical View
As It Was in the Beginning, So Shall It Be...
Daniel In Babylon – The Study Guide
Principles for Victorious Living Volume II
Principles for Victorious Living Volume I
Present Truth Lifestyle – Daniel In Babylon
Esther: Present Truth Church
The Fortress Church
Called to be An Apostle – An Autobiography
Leaven Revealed
Five Pillars of The Apostolic
Apostolic Purity
Apostolic Reformation
Jesus Christ The Apostle and High Priest of Our Profession
Kingdom Advancing Prayer Volume I
Kingdom Advancing Prayer Volume II
Kingdom Advancing Prayer Volume III
Internal Reformation
God's Nature Expressed Through His Names
"I Will Build My Church." – Jesus Christ
Identifying and Defeating the Jezebel Spirit

CONTENTS

INTRODUCTION

Before we launch into this book, let me quote this very important passage of Scripture: Hebrews 11:1-6

Now faith is the substance of things hoped for, the evidence of things not seen. For by it the elders obtained a good testimony. By faith we understand that the worlds were framed by the word of God, so that the things which are seen were not made of things which are visible. By faith Abel offered to God a more excellent sacrifice than Cain, through which he obtained witness that he was righteous, God testifying of his gifts; and through it he being dead still speaks. By faith Enoch was taken away so that he did not see death, "and was not found, because God had taken him"; for before he was taken he had this testimony, that he pleased God. But without faith it is impossible to please Him, for he who comes to God must believe that He is, and that He is a rewarder of those who diligently seek Him.

So, this is the premise from which this book would be written. We cannot even begin to understand the Scriptures or the heart of God if we do not believe that He is. And to do that we must enact the faith that everyone of us were given at birth according to: Romans 12:3

For I say, through the grace given to me, to everyone who is among you, not to think of himself more highly than he ought to think, but to think soberly, as God has dealt to each one a measure of faith.

Because God always existed, we must understand and believe that He existed outside of space and time in the realm called *Eternal*. I believe that this is why we could understand the following passage of Scripture: Matthew 25:34-40

Then the King will say to those on His right hand, 'Come, you blessed of My Father, inherit the kingdom prepared for you from the foundation of the world: for I was hungry and you gave Me food; I was thirsty and you gave Me drink; I was a stranger and you took Me in; I was naked and you clothed Me; I was sick and you visited Me; I was in prison and you came to Me.' "Then the righteous will answer Him, saying, 'Lord, when did we see You hungry and feed You, or thirsty and give You drink? When did we see You a stranger and take You in, or naked and clothe You? Or when did we see You sick, or in prison, and come to You?' And the King will answer and say to them, 'Assuredly, I say to you, inasmuch as you did it to one of the least of these My brethren, you did it to Me.'

Acts 15:18
Known to God from eternity are all His works.

So, He knew exactly what He was seeking to accomplish, and nothing could take Him by surprise.

And that *time,* as we know it only began when He created it. This was done when He created the Heavens and the earth as recorded in the book of Genesis, when He established the sun and the moon and day and night causing, the establishment of days and night, and the record of days.

Here is a thought: What happens to today when it passes and becomes yesterday? Where does it go? Where is tomorrow? I would think that only the Creator, God would be able to effectively answer these questions.

Let us now get into the depth of this book, which we pray would be a source of Divine revelation.

CHAPTER ONE
SPIRITUAL WARFARE
AND GOD'S DIVINE COUNCIL

I WOULD LIKE TO SUBMIT TO YOU THAT CREATION BEGAN WITH THE HEAVENLY Host of the Angels and God's Divine Council and from there the creation of mankind. Let us delve a bit deeper into this statement. I would like to begin with spiritual warfare because this gives us a much clear understanding of the importance of God's Divine Council.

SPIRITUAL WARFARE
For the next few pages, we are going to be talking about spiritual warfare. By "spiritual warfare," I mean battling with "spirit beings," who are non-physical, non-humans. They are supernatural beings. I believe that this would set the tone for us to explore the whole issue of a Divine Council. So, let's get started.

Paul put it this way: Ephesians 6:12 NASB

For our struggle is not against flesh and blood, but against the rulers, against the powers, against the world forces of this darkness, against the spiritual forces of wickedness in the heavenly places.

This is speaking about a battle with spiritual forces, who are not flesh and blood.

When it comes to spirit beings such as satan, the devil, demons, and unclean spirits there are basically three positions or views.

1. Some Believers don't believe in a personal devil or demons; to them there is no such thing.
2. Some believe that satan, demons, and unclean spirits are real beings that are still very active today.
3. Some believe that satan, demons, and unclean spirits are real beings, but were all defeated and destroyed in AD 70 at the return of Christ when the destruction of the Temple and judgment took place.

Those who hold to view 1:

Hold the idea that satan is not a real spiritual being, but instead is merely referring to a personification of sinfulness in the human heart, or to wicked human beings. They would say that satan is merely our own internal sinful human nature or inclination to sin. How would that view fit with Scripture?

Let's start by looking at a verse from the Tanakh, the Old Testament:

Deuteronomy 32:17 NASB
They sacrificed to demons who were not God, To gods whom they have not known, New gods who came lately, Whom your fathers did not dread.

- Here "demons," the Hebrew word shed, are called gods, this is the Hebrew elohim.
- Here "God" is Eloahh, and "gods" is also elohim.
- So, demons are also called elohim.

Michael H. Heiser, the Jewish scholar says, *"Elohim* is a place of residence term." He meant that *elohim* is only used of those in the spirit world. So, in this verse "demons" are called elohim, meaning they are spirit beings, they are not sinful human nature. Do you understand this? Are you able to see this?

Let's move to the New Testament: Matthew 4:1 NASB

*Then Jesus was led up by the Spirit into the wilderness to be tempt-
ed by the devil.*

Question that needs to be answered: If we say that devils and demons
never existed then was Jesus being tempted by His own sinful nature? To
go there is an attack on the deity of Christ.

The Bible teaches that Christ was sinless: Philippians 2:7 NASB

*but emptied Himself, taking the form of a bond-servant, and being
made in the likeness of men.*

Here the word "likeness" is *homoioma*, which suggests similarity, but
different. Though His humanity was genuine, He was different from all
other humans in that He was sinless.

We see this same Greek word in: Romans 8:3 NASB

*For what the Law could not do, weak as it was through the flesh,
God did: sending His own Son in the likeness of sinful flesh and as
an offering for sin, He condemned sin in the flesh.*

Christ came in the "likeness" of sinful flesh. Likeness is from *homoioma*, meaning "similar, but different."

The difference was that He wasn't sinful. Jesus had real human flesh
He felt pain, sorrow, wept, died, but He was sinless: 2 Corinthians 5:21
NASB

*He made Him who knew no sin to be sin on our behalf, so that we
might become the righteousness of God in Him.*

Christ knew no sin: Hebrews 4:15 NASB

*For we do not have a high priest who cannot sympathize with our
weaknesses, but One who has been tempted in all things as we are,
yet without sin.*

Jesus can't be tempted by His own sinful nature because He didn't
have a sinful nature.

Is Christ being tempted by wicked human beings? Most would say that Christ's adversaries were the Jews.

Question then: Could satan here represent the Jews?

Matthew 4:8-10 NASB

Again, the devil took Him to a very high mountain and showed Him all the kingdoms of the world and their glory; and he said to Him, "All these things I will give You, if You fall down and worship me." Then Jesus said to him, "Go, satan! For it is written, 'YOU SHALL WORSHIP THE LORD YOUR GOD, AND SERVE HIM ONLY.'"

Would the Jews at that time ask Christ to worship them? No! Is Christ carrying on a conversation here with Himself? Throughout the text "the tempter" or "the devil" is given personal attributes and clearly distinguished from Jesus as being another person.

I mean that nowhere in this context do we get the idea that the devil is merely referring to a sinful human nature of Christ.

It's kind of ridiculous to think that a sinful nature within Christ demanded Christ to worship Christ, and if He did, Christ would give Christ the nations. satan offering Christ the nations is not an empty promise. satan was ruling the nations. Sinful human beings could not make this offer to Christ.

Those who deny the existence of satan or demons want to make everything the result of natural occurrences.

Bishop Lightfoot writes, "Unclean spirits and demonic possession seem to be no more than physical and mental illness."

And they were casting out many demons and were anointing with oil many sick people and healing them. Mark 6:13 NASB

Here we see a contrast between demons and sickness. They were not casting out mental illness.

I think that this first view is unbiblical. I think that modern science has caused many Believers to question or down right deny the spiritual.

To those of the Ancient Near East everything was spiritual, to us nothing is. If someone believes in God and angels, why is it so hard to believe in satan and demons?

View 2 says: satan, demons, and unclean spirits are real beings who are still very active today. As you read through the Gospels you see many encounters with satan and demons: Mark 1:23-24 NASB

And just then there was in their synagogue a man with an unclean spirit; and he cried out, saying, "What do we have to do with You, Jesus of Nazareth? Have You come to destroy us? I know who You are the Holy One of God!"

"Unclean," is from the Greek word *akathartos*, which, in this sense, refers to evil.

"Spirit" is from the Greek *pneuma* and here refers to a spirit being spirits don't have physical bodies: Luke 24:39 NASB

See My hands and My feet, that it is I Myself; touch Me and see, for a spirit does not have flesh and bones as you see that I have.

Back in Mark 1, there was an unclean spirit in this synagogue, and he disrupted the service.

Notice the possessive pronoun *"their synagogue."* This indicates that this man was not a regular member of the Capernaum synagogue.

This unclean spirit is what we would call a demon. Demon comes from the Greek *daimonion,* which, according to Thayer, means: "a divine power, deity, divinity":

Mark 1:24 NASB
saying, "What do we have to do with You, Jesus of Nazareth? Have You come to destroy us? I know who You are - the Holy One of God!"

Notice that this demon recognizes both Jesus' humanity and His deity. *"Jesus of Nazareth"* speaks of His humanity; *"Holy One of God"* speaks of His deity.

It's interesting to me that here we are 2,000 years later, and we're still arguing about who Jesus was. The demons got it right, they knew who He was. This was God in the flesh. They knew that. And they also understood that there was nothing they could do to keep Jesus from taking authority over them.

The phrase *"Holy One"* is used in the Tanakh or Old Testament writings of Yahweh. Who is the Holy One of Israel: Psalms 78:40-41 NASB

> *How often they rebelled against Him in the wilderness And grieved Him in the desert! Again and again they tempted God, and pained the Holy One of Israel.*

It is Yahweh who is called the *"Holy One"* or the *"Holy One of Israel."* Calling Christ, "The Holy One" is a clear reference to the deity, by no less than the demons themselves.

In the NASV it appears that this demon asks a question, but this is more of a statement in which he tells the facts, the reason Jesus has come to earth: Mark 1:24 YLT

> *saying, 'Away! what to us and to thee, Jesus the Nazarene? thou didst come to destroy us; I have known thee who thou art the Holy One of God.'*

This demon understood that Jesus had come to destroy them: Matthew 25:41 NASB

> *Then He will also say to those on His left, 'Depart from Me, accursed ones, into the eternal fire which has been prepared for the devil and his angels.*

We'll talk about this more in a few minutes. Mark 1:26 NASB

> *And Jesus rebuked him, saying, "Be quiet, and come out of him!" And throwing him into convulsions, the unclean spirit cried out with a loud voice, and came out of him.*

This demon obeys the words of Jesus.

Here Mark is demonstrating Jesus' authority over the fallen spirit world. Jesus will Himself later point out what this proved: that satan in his strength was being defeated, and that this could only be by the Spirit of God:

Matthew 12:28 NASB
But if I cast out demons by the Spirit of God, then the kingdom of God has come upon you.

In order to really understand how these people would have processed this, you have to understand that in the First Century they saw demonic spirits involved in everything bad.

- If you had a disease, it was a demonic spirit.
- If you had a tragedy, it was a demonic spirit.
- If you had a mental illness, it was a demonic spirit.
- The demons were under every rock.
- They were responsible for everything.
- They understood there is nothing they could do about it.
- They just had to live with it. And it tortured these people.

Just to help you understand how desperate they were, they entered into a practice called "trepanning."

Basically, that meant while the person was alive, if they reached a point of torture where they couldn't stand it any longer, they would take a drill and literally drill a hole into their skull hoping that the demonic spirits would escape out the hole. Now that doesn't sound very pleasant. But it gives you some idea of the level of desperation they lived with.

Historians have dug up the cemeteries from the First Century and found about five percent of the skulls had a hole drilled in them. This was a significant thing to them. Along comes Jesus and now there's the solution! demon gone. End of problem.

And they were just stunned with that. Suddenly Jesus identified Himself as the One who could solve their problems; as the One who could remove the demonic spirits; the One who could deal with the issues in their lives. Mark says that the word about Jesus spread immediately.

What about demons today? Do we need to be worrying about demons?

I'm sure you understand that the answer to those questions will be different depending on who you ask. For example:

In the book, Exposing satan's Devices, Betty Miller says, "Some children are born under a curse and have demons that cause their erratic behavior. Parents are in ignorance as to why some children beat their heads on the floor in rages, scream and yell uncontrollably, bite themselves, or have continual nightmares. Many children do have demons and need to be set free."

I would tend to disagree, it is not some children, but all children that are born under a curse. And it has nothing to do with demons, it is the Adamic sin/curse: Romans 5:12 NASB

Therefore, just as through one man sin entered into the world, and death through sin, and so death spread to all men, because all sinned

Miller also says, "One of the deadliest misrepresentations of the truth of God is that a Christian should not be concerned with thoughts that a demon could be their problem. This is taught within many churches and gives the devil a "field day" to bring fear, mental torment, jealousy, hatred, lust, pride, self-pity, addiction, gluttony and many other forms of bondage, oppression, and defilement."

So please hear me and understand this next point:

Well, I guess that your bad behavior is not your fault, you have a demon. So, you don't need to repent, you need to see an exorcist. I truly believe that as a born-again Believer in Jesus Christ and one who is filled with His Holy Spirit, that the devil and demons are not my problem anymore. The responsibility is now mine to change and mature. It is time for me to fully understand that I have everything that I now need to make the transition. Because it is no longer I that live But Christ Who lives in me...

Televangelist, Bob Larson, said, "I have had my physical appearance duplicated by demons." Really! I like that one. When I act in a rude and thoughtless manner towards my wife, I can tell her, "That wasn't me, it was a demon impersonating me to get me in trouble."

When you think of the Charismatic Movement, you think of speaking in tongues, or Benny Hinn knocking people down, and things like that. But there are some underlying things in the Charismatic worldview that are really very, very terrifying. They have a preoccupation with satan and demons:

A woman who came out of the Charismatic Movement wrote this:

"You know we lived all our life in this movement and one thing dominates that movement, and it is that satan is sovereign. If you get sick, it was the devil. If your child gets sick, it was the devil. The devil made your child sick. And even if your child dies satan somehow got the victory. If your spouse, your husband or your wife gets cancer, that's the devil that did that. If you had an accident, the devil did that. If you lost your job, the devil did that. If things didn't go the way you wanted them to go in your company or your family and you wound up with a loss of job or a divorce —the devil did all of that. The devil has to be bound and so you have got to learn these formulas, because you have got to bind the devil, or he is really going to control everything in your life."

She went on to say, "The devil dominates everything, and he is assisted by this massive force of demons who also have to be dealt with, and you have got to do everything you can to try to overcome these spiritual powers, and they are invisible, and they are fast, and they are powerful, and they are really impossible for you to deal with on any permanent basis, so it is an ongoing, incessant struggle with the devil."

She basically said, "We lived our whole lives thinking that everything that went wrong in the entire universe was basically because of the devil. The devil is really sovereign in everything, and even God, along with us, is really struggling like crazy to overcome the devil."

She also wrote, "I lived with heart palpitations, panic attacks, anxiety, frightening dreams waking up in the middle of the night terrified that the devil might be doing something to my child while he's lying in his bed. Just living in this constant terror of what satan was doing; that when the wrong guy gets elected satan put him there. That when the society goes a certain direction, it is all under the control of satan. satan is really the sovereign of everything, and it is really difficult to get control of him - even God is up there wringing His hands trying to get control of this deal."

Is this what the Bible teaches? No, it teaches that Yahweh is Sovereign. The Scriptures show us that God exercises sovereign rule over the entire physical universe, over plant and animal creation, over the nations of the earth, and over all individuals and angles, including satan: Job 1:8-12 declares:

Then the Lord said to satan, "Have you considered My servant Job, that there is none like him on the earth, a blameless and upright man, one who fears God and shuns evil?" So satan answered the Lord and said, "Does Job fear God for nothing? Have You not made a hedge around him, around his household, and around all that he has on every side? You have blessed the work of his hands, and his possessions have increased in the land. But now, stretch out Your hand and touch all that he has, and he will surely curse You to Your face!" And the Lord said to satan, "Behold, all that he has is in your power; only do not lay a hand on his person."

A common myth is that satan is the source of all our trials, problems, and difficulties. Back in the late 60's and early 70's, Flip Wilson had a saying: "The devil made me do it." And more recently Andrea Yates, the mother that killed her five children, said the same thing. She said that the devil made her do it. Is the devil the cause of all our problems?

Yahweh used satan in the Old Covenant to carry out His will, as we see in Job. But satan never did anything apart from the will of God. Please understand this about the God we serve: If satan could act independently of God, God would not be sovereign.

Alright, so some people don't believe in the devil or demons at all. And then others believe that they are real and are still in battle with them. Then there is the third view that:

View 3:

satan, demons, and unclean spirits are real beings, but were all defeated and destroyed in AD 70 at the return of Christ when the Temple was destroyed, and judgment took place.

The view of many today is that what ever happened in the Gospels and the book of Acts is intended to describe Christianity as it ought to be in every age. So, is it normal for us to have problems with demons?

Let's talk a little about demon possession. This is a big issue today, and something we need to have a grasp on, from a biblical perspective. What does the Bible teach us, the born-again Believer about demon possession?

2 Corinthians 6:14-18

Do not be unequally yoked together with unbelievers. For what fellowship has righteousness with lawlessness? And what communion has light with darkness? And what accord has Christ with Belial? Or what part has a believer with an unbeliever? And what agreement has the temple of God with idols? For you are the temple of the living God. As God has said: "I will dwell in them And walk among them. I will be their God, And they shall be My people." Therefore "Come out from among them And be separate, says the Lord. Do not touch what is unclean, And I will receive you." "I will be a Father to you, And you shall be My sons and daughters, Says the Lord Almighty."

The first thing we need to understand is that most of the New Testament references to demon possession appear in the Gospels and represent the outburst of satanic opposition to God's work in Christ.

We have no reference to demon possession after the book of Acts, and we don't have much reference to it in the latter half of the book of Acts. Can anyone cite a demon possessed person after the book of Acts recorded in Scripture?

We encounter occult practices, magicians, and others who dabble in dark power, but seldom an evil spirit that has taken over a life. We have no reference whatsoever to demon possession in the Epistles, not in any of them. We have no reference in the Old Covenant to demon possession either.

Now I would like for you to carefully consider what I am about to share here: Demon possession seems to be something that happened only during the time of Christ and the Apostles for the purpose of manifesting the power of Christ over the demonic world.

Well, what about all those today who claim to be casting out demons? Do they fit the biblical pattern? The exorcisms in the Bible concerned those clearly recognized as possessed.

The signs of demon possession in the New Testament include speechlessness [Matthew 9:33], deafness [Mark 9:25], blindness [Matthew 12:22], fierceness [Matthew 8:28], unusual strength [Mark 5:4], convulsions [Mark 1:26], and foaming at the mouth [Luke 9:39].

Luke 8:27-29 NASB

And when He had come out onto the land, He was met by a certain man from the city who was possessed with demons; and who had not put on any clothing for a long time, and was not living in a house, but in the tombs. And seeing Jesus, he cried out and fell before Him, and said in a loud voice, "What do I have to do with You, Jesus, Son of the Most High God? I beg You, do not torment me." For He had been commanding the unclean spirit to come out of the man. For it had seized him many times; and he was bound with chains and shackles and kept under guard; and yet he would burst his fetters and be driven by the demon into the desert.

Notice the supernatural strength he exhibited. This man had been bound with chains and fetters, but he had snapped the chains and torn off the fetters, and no one had the strength to subdue him a remarkable demonstration of demonic power.

The exorcisms in the Gospels and in Acts were not nebulous [vague] cases of the demon of drugs, alcohol, postnasal drip, or nicotine demons like we see today. In his book, Diary of an *Exorcist*, Win Worley describes a woman who was possessed by two demons: the demon of "dry hair" and the demon of "oily hair." When she would try to treat her oily hair, the demon of dry hair would take over and vice versa thus tormenting her. Does this fit the Biblical pattern?

You can blame all of your problems and all your sins on demons. You could have the demon of pornography or lying or stealing. This seems to be the trend of our day to blame our problems on someone else. We all seem to want to escape from personal responsibility.

We saw in the text in Mark that the demons are to be destroyed. We see this same idea in Matthew 8:28-29 NASB

And when He had come to the other side into the country of the Gadarenes, two men who were demon-possessed met Him as they were coming out of the tombs; they were so exceedingly violent that no one could pass by that road. And behold, they cried out, saying, "What do we have to do with You, Son of God? Have You come here to torment us <u>before the time</u>?" [Emphasis Author's]

The demons understood the mission of Jesus to destroy them. Notice the final words in this verse "**the time**" presumably the time of judgment at the consummation of the ages.

The destruction of satan and demons was prophesied from the beginning: Genesis 3:15 NASB

And I will put enmity Between you and the woman, And between your seed and her seed; He shall bruise you on the head, And you shall bruise him on the heel.

This is a prophecy of Christ overcoming satan. Peter spoke of this judgment that the demons were to experience: 2 Peter 2:4 NASB

For if God did not spare angels when they sinned, but cast them into hell and committed them to pits of darkness, reserved for judgment.

The Greek word for "destroy" is *luo*, which means: "to loosen, destroy, dissolve, put off." Christ is said to have destroyed the devil and his works. Do you believe the Bible? Colossians 2:15 NASB

When He had disarmed the rulers and authorities, He made a public display of them, having triumphed over them through Him.

According to my Bible, satan is a defeated foe. Jesus the Christ has conquered the devil.

Most Christians believe that satan and his demons will be destroyed, but when does it happen? Most Christians look for this event to happen at a future day when the earth and everything physical is destroyed. Perhaps a review of the Scriptures will help clarify the matter: Romans 16:20 NASB

And the God of peace will soon crush satan under your feet. The grace of our Lord Jesus be with you. [Emphasis Author's]

The Greek word used here for crush is *suntribo*, it means: "to crush completely, i.e., to shatter." When is it that satan is to be crushed completely? It's at the end of the Old Covenant, when the Lord returned in judgment on Israel. Paul said here to the Roman Christians that it would happen "soon." The Greek word translated "soon"' is *tachos*. It is used to mean: "speed, quickness, swiftness, haste."

Remember the hermeneutical principle of audience relevance! Do you think that the Believers at Rome could have conceived of 2,000 plus years as soon? If it was to be some 2,000 plus years, how could He crush him under "**their**" feet? The people to whom this was written are dust now, they have no feet.

So, we need to understand that as a born-again Christian, the devil and demons are not our problem. Hence, we do not have one single record of any of them manifesting within the bible after the middle of the book of Acts. He has been defeated and his full defeat was completely manifested in AD70 destruction of the Old Covenant Temple.

In our next chapter we would be delving into God's Divine Council and what the Scriptures say about this.

Let's check our understanding of the chapter "Spiritual Warfare & God's Divine Council."

1. What is meant by "Spiritual Warfare"?

2. How does Scripture explain this phenomenon?

3. What are the three largely held beliefs/positions in relation to Spirit beings? ie: satan, the devil, demons, and unclean spirits

4. How will the view that satan is not a real being but man's sinful nature, hold against Deuteronomy 32:17 or Matthew 4:1?

5. Why is this view flawed? Explain

6. What does the Greek word "homoioma" translated likeness mean?

7. What is this difference that is spoken of in these Scriptures? Explain with Scriptural reference/s.

8. Which Scriptures speak against the idea that Jesus was tempted by wicked human beings?

9. What are the Greek words translated "evil" and "spirit" in Mark 1:23-24 and what are their meanings?

10. How will the meanings of these words change your understanding of this Scripture?

11. What does the Greek word "daimonion" translated demon mean?

12. What is significant about Mark 1:24? What does it reveal to us?

13. Who is referred to as the "Holy One" in the Old Testament?

14. Which Scripture/s depicts Jesus' authority over satan and his angels?

15. What are some of the underlying things of the charismatic worldview that do not corroborate with Scripture?

16. What are the main signs of demon possession recorded in the Bible?

17. Why is it not biblical for us to blame satan and his demons for all of our sins?

18. How will you explain Colossians 2:15 and Romans 6:20

19. What is our responsibility as born-again Believers of Christ, in dealing with the issue of satan, demons and spirit beings?

20. Do you believe that Jesus fully defeated satan when He died, rose again, ascended to heaven and took His place as sovereign King over earth?

CHAPTER TWO
YAHWEH'S DIVINE COUNCIL

EPHESIANS 6:10-12

Finally, my brethren, be strong in the Lord and in the power of His might. Put on the whole armour of God, that you may be able to stand against the wiles of the devil. For we do not wrestle against flesh and blood, but against principalities, against powers, against the rulers of the darkness of this age, against spiritual hosts of wickedness in the heavenly places.

When dealing with spiritual warfare, I believe that there are three positions that are held by Believers on satan and demons.

View 1:

Some do not believe that satan, demons, and unclean spirits are real spirit beings, to them there is no such thing, not now nor was there ever.

View 2:

Others believe that satan, demons, unclean spirits are real spirit beings and are still very active today.

View 3:

And still there are others who believe that satan, demons, and unclean spirits are real beings, but were all defeated and destroyed in AD 70 at the return of Christ when the judgment took place.

But I must say that it was Apostle Axel Sippach who started me down this path. When he came to visit with me after my time in the hospital, we were having conversation and he sort of stumped me when he said that he believed that God had a Divine Council in answer to one of my questions, and it was from that conversation that I began researching the topic. It has been an interesting study. So here we go.

Let's start with our text in Ephesians and let me show you what I believe and why: Ephesians 6:10-12 NASB

Finally, be strong in the Lord and in the strength of His might. Put on the full armor of God, so that you will be able to stand firm against the schemes of the devil. For our struggle is not against flesh and blood, but against the rulers, against the powers, against the world forces of this darkness, against the spiritual forces of wickedness in the heavenly places.

First of all, notice that Paul says that this struggle is "*NOT against flesh and blood.*" In the Greek this is literally, "blood and flesh."

Is Paul saying this is not a physical battle but a philosophical one? That is the view of those who hold to view 1; they do not believe in a personal devil or demons, so this battle is not a spiritual one. But if you look at the four other uses of this phrase, it is referring to humanity vs the spiritual:

Matthew 16:17 NASB
And Jesus said to him, "Blessed are you, Simon Barjona, because flesh and blood did not reveal this to you, but My Father who is in heaven.

This was not a human understanding; it was revelation from the Father: Also, in Galatians 1:16 NASB we see this same idea.

to reveal His Son in me so that I might preach Him among the Gentiles, I did not immediately consult with flesh and blood,

Does this mean that Paul didn't consult with human philosophy? No, he didn't talk to other people about what God had called him to do. The sense of "flesh and blood" is clearly, as the comparison of all these passages shows, "mere human power."

So, in Ephesians 6 I see Paul as saying that their struggle is not with humanity, not with mere human power. So, what is the struggle with? Paul says it is, "against the rulers, against the powers, against the world forces of this darkness, against the spiritual forces of wickedness in the heavenly places." We know what he is saying here; the question is what does he mean?

The word "***rulers***" is from the Greek *arche*, which has a wide range of meanings: "chief [in various applications of order, time, place or rank]:—beginning."

The word "***powers***" is from *exousia*, which means: "power, ability, privilege." These titles are used of human and spiritual powers, but notice the rest of the verse, "against the world forces of this darkness, against the spiritual forces of wickedness in the heavenly places.

"***World forces***" comes from the Greek *kosmokrator*, which, according to *Strong's Concordance* means: "a *world ruler*, an epithet of satan."

Thayer's says it means: "lord of the world, prince of this age, the devil and his demons." This is its only use in the New Testament.

Paul goes on to say, "against the spiritual forces of wickedness in the heavenly places"—these forces are "spiritual," they are not human, and they are in "heavenly places," which denotes the spiritual realm, the place where God dwells. Notice what Paul says in: Colossians 1:16 NASB

For by Him all things were created, both in the heavens and on earth, visible and invisible, whether thrones or dominions or rulers or authorities—all things have been created through Him and for Him.

The phrase "*all things*" occurs six times in Colossians 1:15-20, and literally means: "the all" or "the totality" referring to The Creation.

Jesus designed all creation "visible" [that is, earthly kingdoms and empires] and "invisible" [that is, the angelic principalities and powers].

The words "thrones," "powers," "rulers" and "authorities" probably refer to spirit beings and not to human government. In part, this refers to the hierarchy of spiritual beings.

So, who are these rulers and powers in the Heavens? I believe these are divine beings who were once part of **God's Divine Council**. The idea of a divine council may sound strange to you because most Christians today simply view God as ruling, and satan as opposing Him. God is seen as the only good deity, and satan is seen as the only bad deity. But in the Hebrew Bible we see a divine council, a ruling body consisting of God as the supreme monarch and various supernatural attendants.

All ancient Mediterranean cultures had some conception of a divine council. But the Hebrew Bible describes a divine council under the authority of Yahweh, the God of Israel. While the divine council of Israel and its neighbour share significant features, the divine council of the Israelite religion was distinct in many important ways. Yahweh is a unique God, but He is not alone.

Psalms 82:1 NASB
God takes His stand in His own congregation; He judges in the midst of the rulers.

"*His own congregation*"—is referring to the divine council. "Congregation" is from the Hebrew *edah,* and means: "a stated *assemblage* [specifically a *concourse,*] or generally *a family.*"

The term "divine council" is used by Hebrew Bible scholars to refer to the "heavenly host" [the pantheon of divine beings who administer the affairs of the cosmos].

It is the consensus among ANE [Ancient Near Eastern] scholars that every society from the time of the ancient Sumerians to the time of the Babylonians and the Greeks believed in a pantheon of gods.

Here "God" and "rulers" are both the Hebrew word *elohim*; this is speaking of the divine council, or the "watchers," as Daniel calls them. Speaking of the judgment on Nebuchadnezzar, notice what Daniel says:
Daniel 4:17 NASB

This sentence is by the decree of the angelic watchers And the decision is a command of the holy ones, In order that the living may know That the Most High is ruler over the realm of mankind, And bestows it on whom He wishes And sets over it the lowliest of men.

The word "angelic" is not in the Original text. The word "watchers" is used and it is from the Hebrew *yr*, which means: "an angel as guardian." This word is only used by Daniel, and if you look at the two other times, he uses it, you can see these are spiritual beings: Daniel 4:13 NASB

I was looking in the visions in my mind as I lay on my bed, and be-hold, an angelic watcher, a holy one, descended from heaven.

Every time Daniel uses the term "watchers" he tells us that they are holy ones.

And here he also says that they are from Heaven. Daniel 4:17 says, *"This sentence is by the decree of the angelic watchers And the decision is a command of the holy ones."*

This judgment was by the decree of the watchers; it was a decision that the holy ones made. How many times have you read this verse and never stopped to ask, "Who are the watchers and why are they making decisions?" They are part of Yahweh's divine council. Back to Psalm 82:6

I said, "You are gods, And all of you are sons of the Most High.

Here "gods" is *elohim*. Yahweh, speaking to His divine council, said, "You are gods." But notice the next verse: Psalms 82:7 NASB

Nevertheless <u>you will die like men</u> And fall like any one of the princ-es. [Emphasis Author's]

Compared with Yahweh as *Elohim*, the elohim of the nations were nothing. Yahweh reviewed their performance as "gods" and judges of the gentiles and condemned them for failing to rule justly.

Question: If these *elohim* were men as many have taught, why would Yahweh say, *"You will die like men"*? Yahweh is saying here that He will judge the disobedient watchers—are you seeing this?

All uses of *elohim* in the Tanakh refer to spiritual beings.

Elohim is ONLY used of those in the spirit world, so if they are called elohim, they are not of the physical realm, they are spirit beings.

Many takes Psalm 82 as referring to human rulers, but as I said, *elohim* is never used of living humans, and if we look at Jesus' quote of Psalm 82:6, it will help us see that it is not talking about human rulers. Jesus startles His audience with the claim: John 10:30-33 NASB

I and the Father are one. The Jews picked up stones again to stone Him. Jesus answered them, "I showed you many good works from the Father; for which of them are you stoning Me?" The Jews answered Him, "For a good work we do not stone You, but for blasphemy; and because You, being a man, make Yourself out to be God."

If the "gods" in Psalm 82 were merely human judges and not divine watchers, then Jesus' appeal to this text to defend His claim to deity would make no sense! They, being Jews, certainly would not seek to stone Him as a blasphemer if He appealed to a text about human judges. Jesus seems to be rebuking the Jews for allowing the existence of *elohim* other than the Father but would not accept His claim to be Elohim.

Psalm 89 teaches us that this council is in the heavens, not on earth: Psalms 89:5-7 NASB.

The heavens will praise Your wonders, O LORD; Your faithfulness also in the assembly of the holy ones. For who in the skies is comparable to the LORD? Who among the sons of the mighty is like the LORD, A God greatly feared in the council of the holy ones, And awesome above all those who are around Him?

Let me just say a word here about "Yahweh," which is translated here as "LORD." Once you understand the idea of a "divine council," this covenant name of God becomes so much more important!

God is applying a plumb line to His Church during this current international pandemic. And know this that a plumb line is never ever linear but it is horizontal. So Heaven is dropping a plumb line upon the Church. And know that we are being examined, so let us stand firm and strong in the Lord.

This season is a test. This is not the time to become cynical but a time to know the heart of God and for us to seek His Face!

God is both seeking and is depending on His people to bring Heaven to earth during this time of crisis. Be a solution to someone's confusion. God and His people are true problem solvers. Yes, that is who we are. We are designed to bring Heaven's solutions to the earth!

And we need to understand God's way of bringing Heaven to earth. It is not according to the earth's standards. For example, He has His Davidic people that He is going to use in this time of crisis. You all remember the story of Saul's mighty men who could not deal with Goliath, but it was David a little, ruddy Shepherd boy to deal with Goliath. Even in the Church today we judge strength by size, finance, etc... but God does not judge things that way. We also have Gideon who started out with an impressive 32,000 but in God's economy all that was needed was 300.

I am telling you in this pandemic God is seeking to use one of the 7000 that no one knows about. Could we be one of them?

This is the hour and season for our hearts to be turned to the Lord. Allow the Lord to use you. Be that willing vessel in this season.

God is changing the wine skin of the Church. I believe that the Church is changing, and that change would be forever. We have marginalized the small, house churches and we have glamorized the large churches. Everyone desires to have a big, large church. But I am telling you there is a dimension where Jesus is once again walking with the12s and the 70s— are you hearing me!

I believe that God is using us to make sure that we are raising up an Army and not just an Audience—oh are you hearing me today.

My prayer is that all of you would be students of the Word and movers and shakers in this hour. That you will all become versed in the Ways and things of God. Because you have learnt how to seek the Face and Heart of God.

John Maxwell made this very important statement - We the Church must learn how to adjust our way to victory. We may not be there yet but as we journey to that place, we would need to adjust our way. And that during a crisis "Authenticity is Required" we cannot fake our way through this crisis. We need to be real. This is not the time to rise and make a false claim of victory, but we better know for certain that we must be authentic, because any fake will be easily discerned and exposed.

Remember Daniel and Joseph in this hour of crisis.

So, as we continue to navigate this pandemic let us remain true to God and to each other. Let us be authentic!!!

There are many gods, but Yahweh is God of gods: Deuteronomy 10:17 NASB

For the LORD your God is the God of gods and the Lord of lords, the great, the mighty, and the awesome God who does not show partiality nor take a bribe.

This text says, "For Yahweh your [speaking to Israel] *Elohim* is the Elohim of elohim and the Adonay of adon, the great, the mighty, and awesome El who does not show partiality nor take a bribe." So, there are many gods, but only one Yahweh, who is God of gods: Isaiah 37:16 NASB

O LORD of hosts, the God of Israel, who is enthroned above the cherubim, You are the God, You alone, of all the kingdoms of the earth. You have made heaven and earth.

Yahweh is the Elohim of Israel, and of all the kingdoms of the earth.

Back to Psalm 89: This divine council is in the "skies," this is the Hebrew word *shachaq*, which means: "clouds or heaven."

The divine council is in the Heavens, not on earth where the Jewish judges are. This is not an earthly, human council.

The word "council" here is from the Hebrew *sod*, which means: "a *session*, that is, *company* of persons [in close deliberation]; by implication *intimacy*, *consultation*, a *secret:*—assembly."

These texts in Psalms clearly depict a heavenly council ["in the skies"] and not, as some scholars suggest, a council of earthly human judges.

Psalms 103:19-21 NASB
The LORD has established His throne in the heavens, And His sovereignty rules over all. Bless the LORD, you His angels, Mighty in strength, who perform His word, Obeying the voice of His word! Bless the LORD, all you His hosts, You who serve Him, doing His will.

Here the council members are called "His angels, Mighty in strength" and "His hosts." Are you seeing this? Very interesting.

Throughout the Scriptures we see many different names used of these council members.

- They are called, "the rulers" and "sons of the Most High" in Psalm 82.
- They are called "the watchers" in Daniel 4.
- They are called "the holy ones" and "sons of the Mighty" in Psalm 89.
- They are called *"Sons of God" in Genesis 6, Job 1-2.

- They are called "cherubim" in Genesis 3:24; Exod 25:18-22; Ezekiel 10:1-20.
- They are called "seraphim" in Isaiah 6.
- They are also called "messengers of God" and messengers of Yahweh in numerous places.

Other indications of the council use plural pronouns and verbs in statements attributed to God.

*SONS OF GOD

There are two references to this term and could be very confusing if not understood correctly. Let me seek to explain this:

First we have the "Sons of God" that were created before mankind. For example—Genesis 6:1-4, Job 1:6. I believe that those are a different category to the "sons [or children] of God" those who have surrendered their lives to Jesus and are walking with God. These are referenced in connection to Jesus Christ, God the Father's Pattern Son. Here is what the Scripture says: Hebrews 1:5-9

For to which of the angels did He ever say: "You are My Son, Today I have begotten You"? And again: "I will be to Him a Father, And He shall be to Me a Son"? But when He again brings the firstborn into the world, He says: "Let all the angels of God worship Him." And of the angels He says: "Who makes His angels spirits And His ministers a flame of fire." But to the Son He says: "Your throne, O God, is forever and ever; A scepter of righteousness is the scepter of Your kingdom. You have loved righteousness and hated lawlessness; Therefore God, Your God, has anointed You With the oil of gladness more than Your companions."

And in Hebrews 2:10-11 we see Jesus bringing many sons into glory. And I do not believe this is *gender* specific, so it can refer to both male and female Christians.

For it was fitting for Him, for whom are all things and by whom are all things, in bringing many sons to glory, to make the captain of their salvation perfect through sufferings. For both He who sanctifies and those who are being sanctified are all of one, for which reason He is not ashamed to call them brethren,

We also read the following in John 1:6-12.

There was a man sent from God, whose name was John. The same came for a witness, to bear witness of the Light, that all men through him might believe. He was not that Light, but was sent to bear witness of that Light. That was the true Light, which lighteth every man that cometh into the world. He was in the world, and the world was made by him, and the world knew him not. He came unto his own, and his own received him not. But as many as received him, to them gave he power to become the sons of God, even to them that believe on his name: KJV

So, getting back to the 'Council Members'. Three of these references to these Council Members occur in Genesis chapters 1-11:

Genesis 1:26 NASB
Then God said, "Let Us make man in Our image, according to Our likeness; and let them rule over the fish of the sea and over the birds of the sky and over the cattle and over all the earth, and over every creeping thing that creeps on the earth."

Genesis 3:22 NASB
Then the LORD God said, "Behold, the man has become like one of Us, knowing good and evil; and now, he might stretch out his hand, and take also from the tree of life, and eat, and live forever."

Genesis 11:7 NASB
Come, let Us go down and there confuse their language, so that they will not understand one another's speech.

From Philo [Philo of Alexandria, also called Philo Judaeus, was a Hellenistic Jewish philosopher who lived in Alexandria, in the Roman province of Egypt. He used philosophical allegory to harmonize Jewish Scripture, mainly the Torah, with Greek philosophy] onward, Jewish commentators generally held that these plurals were used because Yahweh was addressing His divine council.

The early post Apostolic Fathers such as Barnabas and Justin Martyr saw the plurals as a reference to the Trinity. I think that is how most Christians see these plurals. But recent scholars tend to agree with ancient Jewish opinion. F. M. Cross notes: "In both Ugaritic [is an extinct Northwest Semitic language, possibly a western dialect of the Amorite language, known through the **Ugaritic** texts discovered by French archaeologists in 1929] and biblical literature, the use of the first-person plural is characteristic of address in the divine council. The familiar 'we' ... has long been recognized as the plural address used by Yahweh in His council" [Cross, Canaanite Myth,187].

Plurals, such as those in Genesis, are seen in the book of Isaiah. For example: Isaiah 6:1-2 NASB

In the year of King Uzziah's death I saw the Lord sitting on a throne, lofty and exalted, with the train of His robe filling the temple. Seraphim stood above Him, each having six wings: with two he covered his face, and with two he covered his feet, and with two he flew.

Here Yahweh is in His throne room surrounded by His court: Isaiah 6:8 NASB

Then I heard the voice of the Lord, saying, "Whom shall I send, and who will go for Us?" Then I said, "Here am I. Send me!"

Here we see that Yahweh's court was made up of His heavenly servants.

When the council gathers for legal purposes, it is typically called into session with an "address to the Divine Council": Isaiah 1:2 NASB

Listen, O heavens, and hear, O earth; For the LORD speaks, "Sons I have reared and brought up, But they have revolted against Me.

The divine council operates on a cosmic level, governing God's universe! On an earthly plane, governing Israel, and nations; and on an individual level, guiding and protecting the righteous Believer.

The council members do not act as autonomous divinities. There is no question as to who, is Head of the assembly: Yahweh makes decisions, and His council responds. The biblical divine council operates with a radically different dynamic than the Babylonian and Canaanite councils called "Yahwism"—Yahweh alone rules in Heaven in holy splendor.

This is why I believe that satan lost his position forever from this council. he sought to operate autonomously and that was not allowed, so God had to cast him and any of the other angels who wanted that level of rule. God alone rules in this council, the others are there to fulfill His every will and command. That is how it is; any other way cannot and will not work! After all Yahweh alone is God, Creator of Heaven, and earth. There is none like Him and we need to accept that as a fact. Obviously lucifer did not.

The one title of Yahweh that most clearly reflects His position as head of the divine assembly is, "Lord of hosts."

Now, while some scholars believe these "armies" refer to Israel's human hosts, most think that they are celestial battalions, belonging to the Creator.

In the Hebrew Bible, a few select men gain access to the divine council. These visitors are the Prophets.

During their visionary entry into working sessions of the royal throne room, they overhear what the King and His counselors decide to do regarding specific human situations. Such visits or "throne visions" are for the purpose of giving the Prophet a message to announce to His people.

Admission into the divine council chambers was one criterion for being a true Prophet, you must have the ability to both see and to hear the word of the Lord, let's look at the following passage: Jeremiah 23:18 NASB

But who has stood in the council of the LORD, That he should see and hear His word? Who has given heed to His word and listened?

"Council" here is the Hebrew, sod, "a *session*, that is, *company* of persons [in close deliberation]; by implication, *intimacy.*

In 2 Chronicles we get a glimpse into the working of the divine council as God's Prophet, Micaiah, describes a vision of the heavenly council that he had been given in regard to a question posed to him by Ahab, king of Israel and Jehoshaphat, king of Judah: 2 Chronicles 18:18-22 NASB

*Micaiah said, "Therefore, hear the word of the LORD. I saw the
LORD sitting on His throne, and all the host of heaven standing on
His right and on His left. "The LORD said, 'Who will entice Ahab
king of Israel to go up and fall at Ramoth-gilead?' And one said this
while another said that. "Then a spirit came forward and stood before the LORD and said, 'I will entice him.' And the LORD said to him,
'How?' "He said, 'I will go and be a deceiving spirit in the mouth of
all his prophets.' Then He said, 'You are to entice him and prevail
also. Go and do so.' "Now therefore, behold, the LORD has put a deceiving spirit in the mouth of these your prophets, for the LORD has
proclaimed disaster against you."*

Here we see mention of the "host of Heaven" [Hebrew *tzeva' hasha-
mayim*], which stands before God. Clearly this is speaking of angelic beings, including those on the heavenly divine council.

This vision seen by Micaiah shows that Almighty God is in complete
control of events. He only approves the course of action that suits His purpose, which in this case was to bring about the death of evil King Ahab.

Let me show you just a few of the texts that indicate that the "host of
Heaven" is more than just the stars in the night sky:

Nehemiah 9:6 NASB
*You alone are the LORD. You have made the heavens, The heaven of
heavens with all their host, The earth and all that is on it, The seas
and all that is in them. You give life to all of them And the heavenly
host bows down before You.*

"You alone are Yahweh"—LORD here in all caps is from the Hebrew
is; this name includes the verb *(hava)*, meaning: "to exist", and the letter
[*yod*] as a prefix, meaning: "He." So, means: "He exists."

If is a causative verb, it would mean: "He causes to exist." Both are
true, Yahweh is the self-existent One who causes to exist.

Only living creatures can worship Yahweh. Clearly, the "Heavenly
host" here refers to created beings which reside in the Heavens.

Jeremiah 19:13 NASB
*The houses of Jerusalem and the houses of the kings of Judah will be
defiled like the place Topheth, because of all the houses on whose*

rooftops they burned sacrifices to all the heavenly host and poured out drink offerings to other gods.

Here Jeremiah draws a parallel between "the heavenly host," to whom incense was burned, and "other gods," to whom drink offerings were poured out.

This grammatical construction in Hebrew is meant to show that both the "the heavenly host," and the "other gods" are the same. They were "the gods of the nations," the angelic rulers assigned by God over the nations of the earth. We'll talk about this in detail later??

One of the most grievous sins of the ancient Israelites was their continual idolatry. Instead of worshiping the one true God Yahweh, they instead worshiped the inferior "sons of God," the "the Heavenly host."

Deuteronomy 4:19

And beware not to lift up your eyes to heaven and see the sun and the moon and the stars, all the **host of heaven**, *and be drawn away and worship them and serve them [note the progressive decline in the preceding verbs], those which the LORD your God has allotted to all the peoples under the whole heaven. [Emphasis Author's]*

Deuteronomy 17:3

who has gone and served other gods and worshiped them, either the sun or moon or any of the host of heaven, which I have not commanded,

In our next chapter we would like to explore what God has to reveal concerning the watchers, the serpent and the shiny one.

Let's check our understanding of the chapter "Yahweh's Divine Council."

1. What are the viewpoints held by Believers on satan and demons when dealing with Spiritual Warfare?

2. What are the Greek words translated rulers, powers, world forces in Ephesians 6:12?

3. Who do you believe are these rulers, thrones, authorities, and powers in heaven as referred to in Colossians 1:15-20?

4. Do you agree the Hebrew "edah" translated "congregation" in Psalm 82:1 was referring to a divine council?

5. How do the Hebrew bible scholars use the term "divine council"?

6. How did Daniel address "God" and "rulers", both words translations of Hebrew "Elohim", in Daniel 4:17?

7. Can you find the word "angelic" in the original manuscripts of the Scriptures Daniel 4:13&17?

8. Every time Daniel speaks of "watchers" what characteristic about these watchers does he emphasize on?

9. Which Scriptures can you find where Prophet Daniel alluding to the "watchers" as "holy ones"?

10. Do you believe these "elohim" translated "gods" in Psalm 82:6 are men? Why or Why not? Explain

11. What is it that God expects of us as His called-out people upon this earth?

12. What is the Hebrew word translated "skies" in Psalms 89:6 and what is its meaning?

13. In Psalm 89:7 what is the Hebrew word translated "council"? What does it mean?

14. Is there Scriptural proof to suggest that this council is not referring to human judges? Explain.

15. What are the many different names used in Scripture to describe the members of this heavenly council?

16. What are the 2 opinions in relation to the use of plurals in statements attributed to God?

17. How does the divine council operate in the 3 distinct levels of Cosmic, Earthly and Individual?

18. Who are the few select men given access/visionary entry to the divine council sessions and for what purpose?

19. What is the Hebrew word translated "council" in Jeremiah 23:18 and how does the meaning of this word tie into your understanding of the Scripture?

20. Which of Israel's many sins could be considered one of the most grievous of all in the eyes of God?

CHAPTER THREE
THE WATCHERS, SERPENT OR SHINY ONE— PART ONE

WE ARE LOOKING AT THE SUBJECT OF SPIRITUAL WARFARE AND PRIMARILY FOCUSING on verse 12 of Ephesians 6

Ephesians 6:12 NASB
For our struggle is not against flesh and blood, but against the rulers, against the powers, against the world forces of this darkness, against the spiritual forces of wickedness in the heavenly places.

This text clearly tells us that they were in a spiritual battle with spiritual powers in the heavens that opposed God and His people. The language in this verse points to a battle that is not physical, but spiritual.

Previously I asked, "Who are these non-flesh and blood world forces of darkness, spiritual forces of wickedness in the heavenly places?" And I said, "I believe these are divine beings who were once part of **God's Divine Council.**"

The idea of a divine council may sound strange to you because most Christians today have never even heard of it. But, hopefully, I demonstrated that in the Hebrew Bible we see a divine council, a ruling body consisting of Yahweh as the supreme monarch and various supernatural attendants.

John the Baptist's father, Zacharias, had a conversation with one of these council members in:

Luke 1:19 NASB
The angel answered and said to him, "I am Gabriel, who stands in the presence of God, and I have been sent to speak to you and to bring you this good news."

LET US TRACK GABRIEL:
The first biblical appearance of Gabriel is in Daniel 8:16, when he is told to explain a vision to the Prophet. He is mentioned twice in Daniel and twice in Luke.

Notice how Gabriel describes himself to Zacharias as, "one who stands in the Presence of God." The Greek word for "stands" is *paristáno*, which means: "to wait before a superior." The *Septuagint* uses this word to describe how Joshua served Moses and how David assisted King Saul.

Later in Luke we read: Luke 1:26 NASB

Now in the sixth month the angel Gabriel was sent from God to a city in Galilee called Nazareth,

Here Gabriel is bringing word to Mary about the birth of Jesus.

When Daniel meets Gabriel, he is frightened and falls on his face. When Gabriel greets Zacharias, his first words are, "Do not be afraid." Mary's greeting is more celebratory, but Gabriel still follows up by telling her not to fear. So, there is something about Gabriel's appearance that scares people.

Here is an honest question WHY DOES GOD NEED COUNSELORS in Heaven?" To which I would ask, "Why did God need to create the universe? Why did God need to create man? Why did God need to send his Son to die for the sins of His elect?" What is the answer to all those questions? He doesn't and He didn't! Yahweh is the self-existent One; He doesn't need anything. Whatever He does is not out of need, but choice. Yahweh does not need counselors, but He does have a divine council. Why? Because He chooses to.

We have looked at the idea that God had allotted "the host of Heaven," the watchers, to the peoples of the earth.

However, I would like to try and develop that idea through the first 11 chapters of Genesis.

Genesis 1:1 NASB
In the beginning God created the heavens and the earth.

In Genesis 1, we have the creation account. Now whether this is a physical creation, or a functional creation is not important for our discussion. I lean toward a functional creation, which means God had already created the world at this time.

For example, it is like when He created Adam. Adam was a physical creation but was not functional until God breathe into him the breath of life and he became a living, functional human being. Well, I believe it was the same way with the earth.

When this creation of Genesis one took place, the Divine Council had already been created. The council was in place before the physical creation. In Job 38:4-7, we see God questioning Job in order to prove a point to him. During that interrogation, He asks Job where he was during the creation of the universe:

Job 38:4-7 NASB
Where were you when I laid the foundation of the earth? Tell Me, if you have understanding, Who set its measurements? Since you know. Or who stretched the line on it? "On what were its bases sunk? Or who laid its cornerstone, When the morning stars sang together And all the sons of God shouted for joy?

Here "morning stars" and "sons of God" are names of divine council members. Some folks see "sons of God" as humans, but how were humans at creation? Somebody please explain that to me. We also see this in:

Genesis 1:26 NASB
Then God said, "Let Us make man in Our image, according to Our likeness; and let them rule over the fish of the sea and over the birds of the sky and over the cattle and over all the earth, and over every creeping thing that creeps on the earth."

The use of plural pronouns here is evidence of the council. So, Yahweh had His council before the creation of Genesis 1.

Paul teaches us that Christ is the agent of creation:

Colossians 1:16 NASB
For by Him all things were created, both in the heavens and on earth, visible and invisible, whether thrones or dominions or rulers or authorities—all things have been created through Him and for Him.

In the phrase, *"All things have been created 'through' Him,"* we see that Jesus is the instrument of creation. He is the agent whereby the universe was created. He is the Creator. And creation is designed *"for him."* This is a term of purpose. Creation is designed for the glory of Christ. He is the goal of creation. Christ is glorified in creation.

In the creation account, God creates Adam:

Genesis 1:27 NASB
God created man in His own image, in the image of God He created him; male and female He created them.

We are created, "as" the image of God, would be a better translation. This means that we are divine representatives. We are to represent Him; we are to do what God wants us to do as if He were physically present with us.

So, God creates Adam. And according to Job, Adam had access to the council:

Job 15:7-8 NASB
Were you the first man to be born, Or were you brought forth before the hills? "Do you hear the secret counsel of God, And limit wisdom to yourself?"

The first man, Adam, was in Eden in the council of God. Adam was in an intimate relationship with God.

Genesis 3:8 NASB
They heard the sound of the LORD God walking in the garden in the cool of the day, and the man and his wife hid themselves from the presence of the LORD God among the trees of the garden.

Adam and Eve walked in the garden with God. They dwelt in His presence. Eden is where God lives and issues decrees. He is with His heavenly host, who existed before humanity did. This is the divine council; the family of God, and Adam was there with them.

You know what happens next, man is tempted, and he sins. Who tempted him and why? I don't think it was a snake.

Well, it could not be a member of the animal kingdom as we know snakes today. The Scripture gives us some very clear clues as to who this creature was:

Most people take for granted that a snake tempted Eve. This is due primarily to how most Bibles translate the Hebrew word *Nachash* [Strong's Concordance #H5175], which is used to designate the beast that led her to sin. The KJV and other versions of God's word such as the NKJV, NIV, and NASB translate *Nachash*, found in Genesis 3, as "serpent." Other Bibles, like the CEV translations, state that she was led astray by a "snake."

In modern English, both "snake" and "serpent" mean roughly the same thing. This creature is an elongated reptile that has no limbs and possesses scales. It journeys from place to place by moving its body along the ground. This short study will show that this animal, commonly believed to be the culprit that tempted Eve and bought "the fall of man," is NOT the same one described in the Bible!

The first verse of Genesis 3 introduces to us the "serpent" [snake] allowed in the Garden of Eden with the express purpose of testing the obedience of the first humans, especially Eve.

Genesis 3:1
Now the serpent [Nachash] was more cunning than any beast of the field which the Lord God had made. And he said to the woman, "Has God indeed said, 'You shall not eat of every tree of the garden'?

What does Genesis reveal to us about the unique beast that Satan possessed in order to deceive Eve? Was it really a snake? A straightforward reading of Genesis 2 and 3 tells us the following about the *Nachash*.

- It was an animal created by God [on the same day Adam and Eve were made!] that was declared "very good" [see Genesis 1:24-26, 3:1]. It was even given a name by Adam [2:19–20].
- It was made with a certain amount of reasoning ability ["it was more cunning than any creature . . ."] that was above all other created beasts.
- It could speak to Eve and had the necessary organs to allow it to do so.
- It was able to walk erect and had [at the minimum] at least four limbs.

I want to think that in Genesis 3 we see one of the watchers, a council member, who had fallen along with lucifer tempting man so he could get rid of him.

You see I believe that God had made man **vice-regent** [a person who rules or reigns: GOVERNOR] with Him, and some of the watchers may not have been too happy about this.

I think that it is interesting that in the *Quran* it is said that lucifer rebelled against Allah because he was told to bow down and worship the clay-born "man of earth," Adam, and refused. [1]

There may be some truth to that.

Some of the watchers may have been upset about God's creation of man and His admittance to the council. I asked, "Who tempted him [Adam/mankind] and why?" The "why" we cannot be sure of, but I think we can understand the "who."

Genesis 3:1 NASB
Now the serpent was more crafty than any beast of the field which the LORD God had made. And he said to the woman, "Indeed, has God said, 'You shall not eat from any tree of the garden'?"

So, we see here that it was the "serpent" that tempted them.

---

[1] See article: https://gh.opera.news/gh/en/religion/d5ecb4de07499f6ecee4639b6676a72c

That we know, what we need to know is who or what is the "serpent." I believe that this "serpent" was a divine being, it was not a member of the animal kingdom, but I believe that it could have been a member of the divine council.

This watcher chose to oppose God's plan for humanity by prompting humans to disobey God, so they would either be killed or removed from Eden, God's council, and family.

At the end of the creation account what happens? God rests. What does that mean? Was he tired from creating? No, John Walden, in his book, *The Lost World of Genesis One*, writes, "The difference is the piece of information that everyone knew in the ancient world and to which most modern readers are totally oblivious: Deity rests in a temple, and only a temple" [page 71]. And what we need to see is that Eden compares to tabernacle or Temple, it is God's dwelling where the divine council was.

In ANE culture God dwelt in the best places, a lush garden, an oasis, or a mountaintop. So, Adam was created and brought into God›s dwelling with His council.

A brief understanding of the **ANE**:

The Ancient Near East refers to early civilizations in a region roughly corresponding to the modern Middle East: Mesopotamia [modern Iraq and Syria], Anatolia [modern Turkey], the Levant [modern Syria, Lebanon, Israel, Palestine, and Jordan], as well as Persia [modern Iran], and Ancient Egypt, from the beginnings of Sumer in the 6th millennium BC until the region's conquest by Alexander the Great in the 4th century BC. The Ancient Near East is considered the cradle of civilization. It was the first to practice intensive year-round agriculture; it produced the first writing system, invented the potter's wheel and then the vehicular, and mill wheels, the first centralized governments, law codes and empires, as well as introducing social stratification, slavery, and organized welfare, and it laid the foundation for the fields of astronomy and mathematics.

Let's look at the text in Genesis 3:1, "serpent" here is from the Hebrew word *nachash*, which, according to Hebrew scholar Michael Heiser, is most likely a triple entendre [understanding], which is a word or phrase that has three different meanings at once.

The root of *nachash* is [noon, het and sheen], which is the basis for a noun, a verb, and an adjective in Hebrew. If you take *nachash* as pointing to the noun, the word here will mean: "serpent". This is a valid translation, but you must keep in mind that the "serpent" referenced here is not a member of the animal kingdom.

If you were to take it as a verb, it would mean: "deceiver" or "diviner." So *nachash* could imply a "deceiver." This option also fits the story.

As an adjective it would mean: "bronze," or "the shining one." In our text it is *"ha nachash"* [the Shining one].

Luminosity is a characteristic of a divine being in the Hebrew Bible and in the *ANE* texts, luminosity is not the characteristic of an animal or a man.

This is a divine being, not an animal or man. Would Eve carry on a conversation with a snake? I don't think so, but she would talk to a divine being. We continue with this train of thought in our next chapter with part two.

Let's check our understanding of the chapter "The Watchers, Serpent or Shiny One – Part One."

1. Does the idea of a Divine Council seem strange to you? Explain.

2. As recorded in the Word of God, what were the initial reactions of those who met Gabriel face to face? Why do you believe they reacted the way they did?

3. According to Scripture, did the Sons of God exist before the creation of man?

4. What is the purpose of the creation according to Colossians 1:16?

5. Do you agree that Adam had access to the divine council? Explain with Scriptural references.

6. What were the unique characteristics of the beast that was instrumental in deceiving Eve?

7. Does this description fit the serpent/snake as we know them today?

8. What are the 3 different meanings to the Hebrew word translated "serpent" here in Genesis 3:1?

9. With what does the Hebrew Scripture associate Luminosity?

10. Based on the insight into the affairs of God as was demonstrated in the discussion with Eve, do you agree that this beast could be non-other than a former member of the divine council? Why or why not?

CHAPTER FOUR
THE WATCHERS, SERPENT OR SHINY ONE—
PART TWO

WE ARE BORN FOR SUCH A TIME AS THIS! AND AS SUCH WE MUST CONTINUE TO RISE and meet our calling. This is the season and reason why we were created! We have to believe and know this. We must embrace that we were born for this time and become the sacrifice to our generation.

God always rises up and send someone with a mandate for his/her time. And a lot of the times, that gift do not reap the fruit of that assignment. Because for the most part his/her revelation is fought against and rejected but he/she must stay the course of that assignment and be willing to be sacrificed! Remember men like Martin Luther who brought the Church the truth, that the just shall live by faith! He was rejected and ostracized. So let us be prepared to be misaligned for what has been released to us!

In order for the Church to grow and become all that the Father has ordained for us to be we need these types of Pioneers! Those who will not buckle under the power of new revelation and truth. Those who could stand the challenge, of what is new in God. Even to the point of being willing to walk alone, if need be, in order to maintain the integrity of the move and call of God.

Adam and Eve lived in the Garden of God; they were very familiar with these divine beings. Let's look at Isaiah 6:

Isaiah 6:1-2 NASB

In the year of King Uzziah's death I saw the Lord sitting on a throne, lofty and exalted, with the train of His robe filling the temple. Seraphim stood above Him, each having six wings: with two he covered his face, and with two he covered his feet, and with two he flew.

The word "seraphim" here mean: "the shining" or "blazing ones" [note: seraphim being plural]. We also have the Hebrew *saraph* as the singular, which means: "fiery serpent."

Ok, so let us have another look at Genesis 3:1 NASB

Now the serpent was more crafty than any beast of the field which the LORD God had made. And he said to the woman, "Indeed, has God said, 'You shall not eat from any tree of the garden'?"

[How many of us thought that the Scripture was referring to a snake or serpent, as we have today? But as we take the time to truly consider what this was, we realize from a Hebrew perspective they could not have thought that it was a snake like we know today, but that it was a much deeper meaning] ... Let us dig a bit deeper here!

There are parallels between Genesis 3, Isaiah 14:12-15 and Ezekiel 28:11-19 [which you can read in your study, however, let us read the first two initially].

Genesis 3:1 NASB

Now the serpent was more crafty than any beast of the field which the LORD God had made. And he said to the woman, "Indeed, has God said, 'You shall not eat from any tree of the garden'?"

Isaiah 14:12-15 NASB

"How you have fallen from heaven, O star of the morning, son of the dawn! You have been cut down to the earth, You who have weakened the nations! "But you said in your heart, 'I will ascend to heaven; I will raise my throne above the stars of God, And I will sit on the mount of assembly In the recesses of the north. 'I will ascend above the heights of the clouds; I will make myself like the Most High.' "Nevertheless you will be thrust down to Sheol, To the recesses of the pit.

So, what we have in Genesis 3 is that of a divine being, not an animal, but a throne room guardian, a *saraph*, a serpentine being, one who was part of the divine council in Eden who decided to deceive humanity to get rid of them; to get humans removed from Eden, from God's council and family. Why? I think the Scriptures hint at pride or jealousy.

The passages in Isaiah and Ezekiel are about evil tyrant kings, whose pride is described in terms of an ancient story about a divine being who fell from paradise due to rebellion against God. These accounts reference Eden directly in Ezekiel's case, and indirectly in Isaiah's case.

In Genesis 3 the *nachash* [the serpentine, shining one, deceiver] was in the Garden of Eden where God walked. Notice what Ezekiel says:

Ezekiel 28:13 NASB
You were in Eden, the garden of God; Every precious stone was your covering: The ruby, the topaz and the diamond; The beryl, the onyx and the jasper; The lapis lazuli, the turquoise and the emerald; And the gold, the workmanship of your settings and sockets, was in you. On the day that you were created They were prepared.

These stones elsewhere describe the brightness of God's throne. So, from this account we could deduce that whoever this is talking about is in God's Temple, His throne room.

Ezekiel 28:14 NASB
You were the anointed cherub who covers, And I placed you there. You were on the holy mountain of God; You walked in the midst of the stones of fire.

"Anointed cherub"—anointed is the word [2]mashach, which means: "anointed," but it may also come from a Semitic homonym, "to shine" [The shining cherub]. Cherub and Seraphim are the same, in Assyrian it is a throne guardian. Brown- Driver- Briggs definition is: an angelic being, a guardian of Eden. The "cherub" serpent figure is in the "midst of the stones of fire," which is the divine council. In this text Eden is called a garden and a mountain:

---

[2] Researched from https://www.bibletools.org/index.cfm/fuseaction/Lexicon.show/ID/H4886/mashach.htm

Ezekiel 28:12 NASB

Son of man, take up a lamentation over the king of Tyre and say to him, 'Thus says the Lord GOD, "You had <u>the seal of perfection</u>, Full of wisdom and perfect in beauty." [Emphasis Author's]

Isaiah 14:12 NASB

How you have fallen from heaven, O star of the morning, son of the dawn! You have been cut down to the earth, You who have weakened the nations!

"*O star of the morning, son of the dawn*"—this phrase "*son of the dawn*" is "*Helel ben Shachar*," which means: "the Shining one." lucifer is the Latin vulgate translation of Helel [shining, a luminous being].

Isaiah 14:13 NASB

But you said in your heart, 'I will ascend to heaven; I will raise my throne above the stars of God, And I will sit on the mount of assembly In the recesses of the north.

The "mount of the assembly" is the home of God, the place of the divine council. This divine being seeks to usurp God. We already saw in Job 38 that the sons of God are described as the stars.

This being "shining one" talked about in Isaiah 14 and Ezekiel 28 was in Eden, he was a member of the divine council. This being tempts man, and man sins, he falls and is removed from God's Temple.

He is put out of the Garden. But then we have a promise from God:

Genesis 3:15 NASB

And I will put enmity Between you and the woman, And between your seed and her seed; He shall bruise you on the head, And you shall bruise him on the heel.

Eve's seed, a human being, will come and fix what Adam has done. A Deliverer will come. But for now, man is banished from the presence of God.

Even though man is removed from the Garden Temple, God is still communicating with man. Notice these three very important verses:

Genesis 5:22 NASB
Then Enoch walked with God three hundred years after he became the father of Methuselah, and he had other sons and daughters.

Genesis 5:24 NASB
Enoch walked with God; and he was not, for God took him.

Genesis 6:9 NASB
These are the records of the generations of Noah. Noah was a righteous man, blameless in his time; Noah walked with God.

"*Walked with God*"—is a very significant phrase. This phrase only occurs three times in the Bible and none in the New Testament. When God walks with men, it is a really rare thing. The first occasion of this was in Genesis 3, "*LORD God walking in the garden*." Adam was in that Garden, Adam walked with God in that Garden/Temple. Walking with God depicts a direct divine encounter, a direct divine relationship.

Sometimes we think that the people from Adam to Abraham were ignorant of God and His ways, but these men walked with God, they knew Him:

Genesis 7:1-2 NASB
Then the LORD said to Noah, "Enter the ark, you and all your household, for you alone I have seen to be righteous before Me in this time. "You shall take with you of every clean animal by sevens, a male and his female; and of the animals that are not clean two, a male and his female."

Anything strike you as interesting in these verses? How did they know "clean" and "unclean" animals? The Law wasn't given until fourteen hundred years later. These men knew God, they had been given laws. They were in a relationship with Him. And God was already laying the foundation for His Master Plan to restore mankind—Genius!

Enoch and Noah are God's Prophets according to Jude and Peter:

Jude 1:14 NASB
It was also about these men that Enoch, in the seventh generation from Adam, prophesied, saying, "Behold, the Lord came with many thousands of His holy ones,

2 Peter 2:5 NASB
and did not spare the ancient world, but preserved Noah, a preacher of righteousness, with seven others, when He brought a flood upon the world of the ungodly.

As earth's population grows it becomes wicked as a result of a divine rebellion as per Genesis 3 and 6. Man begins to worship the watchers instead of the watcher's creator, God.

This rebellion of man culminates in building a ziggurat or tower at Babel: Genesis 11:8-9 NASB

So the LORD scattered them abroad from there over the face of the whole earth; and they stopped building the city. Therefore its name was called Babel, because there the LORD confused the language of the whole earth; and from there the LORD scattered them abroad over the face of the whole earth.

Things are in a state of chaos. They are in rebellion against God, and they are judged. They will not follow Him, so He disburses them and turns them over to lesser deities.

So, at this stage Yahweh, is the God of the whole earth! But mankind begins to rebel against the true and living God. So, God decided to scatter them and assign the lesser deities to rule over them. He has a plan...

Genesis 11:8-9 is a very significant text, which we learn more about in: Deuteronomy 32:8 NASB gives us more insight!

When the Most High gave the nations their inheritance, When He separated the sons of man, [Adam] He set the boundaries of the peoples According to the number of the sons of Israel.

The English translations based on the traditional Hebrew text of the *Tanakh* read "sons of Israel." But there is a variant rendering of this passage. It's based on the 3rd-century BC [Before Christ] or BCE [Before Common Era] translation of the Hebrew Scriptures into Greek, the *Septuagint*, as well as Hebrew manuscripts of Deuteronomy found among the Dead Sea Scrolls at Qumran:

Deuteronomy 32:8 RSV
When the Most High gave to the nations their inheritance, when He separated the sons of men, He fixed the bounds of the peoples according to the number of the SONS OF GOD.

Here is another *translation of the Septuagint into English:*

Deuteronomy 32:7-8 KJV
Remember the days of old, consider the years for past ages: ask thy father, and he shall relate to thee, thine elders, and they shall tell thee. 8 When the Most High divided the nations, when He separated the sons of Adam, He set the bounds of the nations according to the number of the angels of God.

Deuteronomy 32:7-8 NLT
Remember the days of long ago; think about the generations past. Ask your father, and he will inform you. Inquire of your elders, and they will tell you. When the Most High assigned lands to the nations, when he divided up the human race, he established the boundaries of the peoples according to the number in his heavenly court.

In the *Septuagint* the Greek phrase *"aggelon theou"* is translated: "angels of God." This interpretive phrase is found in nearly all the existing *Septuagint* manuscripts. However, several earlier manuscripts have instead *"huion theou,"* or "sons of God." This is a literal rendering of the Hebrew phrase *beney 'elohim* found among the *Dead Sea Scroll* copies of Deuteronomy 32:8.

The *Septuagint* translators plainly understood that the "sons of God" [beney 'elohim] spoken of in Deuteronomy 32:8 and elsewhere were spirit beings ["angels"] and rendered it that way several times (Job 1:6; 2:1; 38:7) in order to clarify the meaning. Thus, the textual change from *"huion theou"* to *"aggelon theou."*

In Genesis 10, the table of nations, God divides Noah's descendants into 70 different nations. This is recorded in:

Genesis 10:32 NASB

These are the families of the sons of Noah, according to their gene-alogies, by their nations; and out of these the nations were separat-ed on the earth after the flood.

Chapter 10 of Genesis is the backdrop for Moses' statement in Deuteronomy 32:8 that God is responsible for the creation and placement of the nations [Hebrew goyim]. In fact, variations of the same Hebrew root word *parad* ["separate"] are used in both Genesis 10:32 and Deuteronomy 32:8.

The idea that the separation of mankind into 70 nations at the Tower of Babel was by God and for the angelic "sons of God".

This is supported by the ancient *Book of Jasher*, with reference being made to in two books of our current Bible [It is mentioned in Joshua 10:13, *"Is it not written in the book of Jasher?"* and 2 Samuel 1:18, *"it is written in the book of Jasher."*]

This book of Jasher is made up of 91 chapters. The translation "Book of the Just Man" is the traditional Greek and Latin translation, while the transliterated form "Jasher" is found in the King James Bible, up to year 1611. As to why it was excluded after year 1611, I have no idea.

It can be sourced here for further reading:[3]

Jasher 9:31-32
And they built the tower and the city, and they did this thing daily until many days and years were elapsed. And God said to the seven-ty angels who stood foremost before him, to those who were near to him, saying, Come let us descend and confuse their tongues, that one man shall not understand the language of his neighbor, and they did so unto them.

If in Deuteronomy 32, Moses was indeed referencing Yahweh's separation of the nations according to Noah's offspring [specifically their

---

[3] https://www.sacred-texts.com/chr/apo/jasher/index.htm

physical separation at the Tower of Babel], it is <u>important to note that Israel is not listed in the index of the 70 nations found in Genesis 10</u>.

The nation of Israel did not yet exist at that time. Therefore, the statement by some that God *"set the boundaries of the nations according to the number of the children of Israel"* clearly seems out of context here.

What happens at Babel is, man's disobedience causes God to divide them up and give them to the lesser gods. They were to worship the lesser gods because God was done with them. Man continued to reject God and serve other lesser gods, so God gave them up. What happens to them is recorded in chapter 12 of Genesis.

Genesis 12:1-2 NASB
Now the LORD said to Abram, "Go forth from your country, And from your relatives And from your father's house, To the land which I will show you; And I will make you a great nation, And I will bless you, And make your name great; And so you shall be a blessing."

God calls Abraham and starts over with Israel as His people. God starts a new family. He has turned over the nations to the lesser gods, who, in fact, work for Him. They are all under His control and He will someday call the nations back.

Deuteronomy 32:8-9 NASB
When the Most High gave the nations their inheritance, When He separated the sons of man, He set the boundaries of the peoples According to the number of the sons of God [Israel]. "For the LORD'S portion is His people; Jacob is the allotment of His inheritance."

These two verses are fundamental for understanding the worldview of Old Covenant Israel. These verses explain both the existence of the foreign pantheons/gods and their inferiority to Yahweh God.

The point of verses 8-9 is that sometime after God separated the people of the earth at Babel and established where on the earth they were to be located, He then assigned each of the seventy nations to the fallen sons of God [who were also seventy in number].

According to Deuteronomy 4:19 this "giving up" of the nations was a punitive act:

Deuteronomy 4:19-20 NASB
And beware not to lift up your eyes to heaven and see the sun and the moon and the stars, all the host of heaven, and be drawn away and worship them and serve them, those which the LORD your God has allotted to all the peoples under the whole heaven. But the LORD has taken you and brought you out of the iron furnace, from Egypt, to be a people of His own possession, as today.

We saw earlier in our study that the "host of Heaven" referred to sentient [that is the ability to perceive or feel things] created spiritual beings, which reside in the Heavens. Notice here in Deuteronomy 4:19 that these "host of Heaven" have been "allotted to the peoples." The word "allotted" in Hebrew is *chalaq,* which literally means: "apportioned" or "assigned." Here we are told that Yahweh has assigned "the host of Heaven" to the peoples of the earth; meaning; "all non-Israelites."

Psalms 46:10
Be still, and know that I am God; I will be exalted among the nations, I will be exalted in the earth!

I believe that this is one of those verses that have eternal significance. And it is much more applicable in this day that we live. God will be exalted! And there is no one or anything that can stop this from occurring. His Kingdom will continue to expand and grow until it fills the entire earth. God WILL BE exalted.

Israel was not to worship the watchers. Speaking of judgment that was to come upon disobedient Israel, Moses says:

Deuteronomy 29:24-27 NASB
All the nations will say, 'Why has the LORD done thus to this land? Why this great outburst of anger?' "Then men will say, 'Because they forsook the covenant of the LORD, the God of their fathers, which He made with them when He brought them out of the land of Egypt. 'They went and served other gods and worshiped them, gods whom they have not known and whom He had not allotted to them. 'Therefore, the anger of the LORD burned against that land, to bring upon it every curse which is written in this book.'

These gods that Israel worshiped were "not allotted to them" those gods were allotted to the nations.

So, at the tower of Babel God is done with the nations, they want to follow and serve the watchers above God. So, God gives the watchers to rule over the nations, and in Chapter 12 He calls Abram/Abraham and starts over with His own people Israel.

At Mt. Sinai God gives Israel, His people the Ten Decalogue or Commandments: Exodus 20:1-2 NASB.

Then God spoke all these words, saying, "I am the LORD your God, who brought you out of the land of Egypt, out of the house of slavery."

What is the very first command He gives them?

Exodus 20:3 NASB
You shall have no other gods before Me.

They would not listen, and they followed after other gods, and God disciplined them.

In reading the book of Deuteronomy I noticed that this phrase kept coming up:

Deuteronomy 1:10 NASB
The LORD your God has multiplied you, and behold, you are this day like the stars of heaven in number.

Deuteronomy 5:6
I am the Lord your God who brought you out of the land of Egypt, out of the house of slavery.

This phrase *"The Lord Your God"* is used 279 times in Deuteronomy, and 161 additional times in the *Tanakh*. Yahweh was Israel's God, and they were to have no other gods before Him.

As we come to the New Testament, we see in Acts 2 at Pentecost that God begins to reclaim all the nations for Himself. God, in other words, had not forever abandoned the nations.

Acts 2:5-13

Now there were Jews living in Jerusalem, devout men from every na-tion under heaven. And when this sound occurred, the crowd came together, and were bewildered because each one of them was hear-ing them speak in his own language. They were amazed and aston-ished, saying, "Why, are not all these who are speaking Galileans? And how is it that we each hear them in our own language to which we were born? Parthians and Medes and Elamites, and residents of Mesopotamia, Judea and Capadocia, Pontus and Asia, Phrygia and Pamphylia, Egypt and the districts of Libya around Cyrene, and vis-itors from Rome, both Jews and proselytes, Cretans and Arabs—we hear them in our own tongues speaking of the mighty deeds of God." And they all continued in amazement and great perplexity, saying to one another, "What does this mean?" But others were mocking and saying, "They are full of sweet wine." [Emphasis Author's]

Even in the Old Covenant, Israel was to be a kingdom of priests, me-diators between the disinherited nations and the true God. Just as we Believers are today. The Church is now the new Israel of God and as such the nations of the earth are to come to God through us.

My wife Sandra and I were discussing aspects of this teaching the thought struck us that we were not given any other names of the arch-angels except for Michael and Gabriel and looking at lucifer and how he was created and the level of his beauty and function that he was possibly another archangel and as such may have authority over 1/3 of the angels. That each archangel could have had 1/3 of the angels, hence the reason for lucifer being able to convince 1/3 of the angels to side with him in rebellion against Yahweh God. But again, we do not have any Scripture to support our thinking.

In the next chapter we would be exploring the creation of Angels and their function.

Let's check our understanding of the chapter "The Watchers, Serpent or Shiny One – Two."

1. According to the author, what is the reason most people are not able to achieve the God given mandate for their lives?

2. How are the two words Hebrew words Seraphim & Seraph translated into English. How are they connected to one another?

3. Do you believe it's possible that Adam and Eve were familiar with these divine creatures? Explain.

4. What is the Hebrew word translated "anointed" in Ezekiel 28:14? What other meanings can this word carry?

5. Where is it this shining, far extending one wanting to establish his throne according to Isaiah?

6. What could have led to this shining one to be cast out of the council/ Temple of God?

7. Which Scriptures show us that even though God banished man from the Garden of Eden where His temple/council met, that God still communicates with man?

8. What is the significance of the phrase "walked with God"?

9. How will you explain God's direction to Noah in Genesis 7:1-2 about how many of each type of animals to take into the ark?

10. Which Scriptures confirm to us that Enoch and Noah were both Prophets of God?

11. What do you believe sparked the idea of building a tower to reach up to the heavens?

12. How will you contract this phenomenon with the reason that the shining cherub satan was banished from God's presence/His divine council?

13. Which manuscripts carry a variant of the Scripture Deuteronomy 32:8? How does it vary from the Tanakh?

14. Who are the 2 Prophets found in the Bible referring to the book of Jasher?

15. Until which year was the book of Jasher a part of the King James translation of the Bible?

16. Why is it not possible that Moses was not referring to "the sons Israel" in Deuteronomy 32:8?

17. What are the 2 Scriptures vital to understanding the world view of Old Covenant Israel?

18. How is dividing the nations according to the number of the sons of God and keeping only Israel as His inheritance a punitive action as implied by Deuteronomy 4:19-20?

19. Who then were to be the deities of the nations except Israel?

20. How many times is the phrase "The Lord Your God" used in the book of Deuteronomy? Do you believe this is of any significance?

21. What was the role that Israel was to play in the lives of those disinherited nations, the role now we as His people are re-assigned?

CHAPTER FIVE
CREATION OF ANGELS

ONE OF THE VERY FIRST THINGS THAT I WOULD LIKE TO TALK ABOUT CONCERNING Angels, is the idea of Yahweh creating them and giving them free will. I say this because of what is recorded concerning them and the idea of lucifer being able to rebel against God and assume control over 1/3 of the Heavenly Host. Let us dig a bit deeper into this.

THE ANGELS
The first thing that the Eternal God did was to create His angelic host. He created lucifer and all the other angels so that they would serve in His Kingdom.

We know that the Creator God is Eternal [meaning He has no beginning or ending] and always was, is very present and always will be. We also know that there is no being above Him or His equal and that no one or anything existed before Him, because He always existed! However, we also know from Scripture that the angels existed before He created what we know to be the "physical heavens and the earth". Hence, He had to create them because He is the only Eternal Being, everyone and everything else has/had a beginning, including lucifer.

Long before time existed, the Godhead was! Three persons; coherent, and co-existing in One—Father, Son and Holy Spirit were there always, longing to share "Love"—the God kind of 'love', agape; in its purest form, the very essence of their being. Permit me to say this: all that the Lord has done/is doing is as a result of whom and what He is, Love, in its purest form!

I remember one time many, many years ago as I was sitting on my bed and as I looked through my window and gazed into the sky, I pondered on who this Awesome God that we serve is. As I sat there, in my mind's eye I removed everything that there was, ending up with what we call space and thinking to myself God existed even before there was space. The more I explored this, I heard the Holy Spirit say to me "if you were to strip away all that you know about God, His omnipresence, His omnipotence, His almightiness, His awesomeness, His majesty, [and the list goes on] you will get to the point where you cannot strip anything else away and you will find out who this God really is, and that would be—pure, perfect and unblemished Love!

As a matter of fact, if we were to do a deeper study of the Hebrew word for God, it means the self-existent one. Yes, God could have existed all by Himself. However, because love is at the very core of His being, He chose not to be by Himself. In fact, He could not because the very nature of love would not permit it. Love is always giving, always sharing, always caring.

LUCIFER'S REVOLT

The strength and essence of this love was demonstrated in the fact that He created the angels including lucifer the cherubim who thought he could dethrone God. God certainly was aware of this but still allowed him to continue.

I am certain that God gave lucifer an opportunity to not take that course of action resulting in banishment, to appreciate the goodness of his Creator and not follow down that road. lucifer paid the price as he and one third of the angels were cast out of Heaven because of their rebellion!

The question could be asked—what caused God to allow lucifer to convince one-third of the angels to him in rebellion against Him? Are you seeing this? In order for one-third of the angels to rebel, lucifer had to speak to all of them. Not only that, but God had to know he was doing it. What could have caused Almighty God to allow that to go on seemingly unchecked? I believe the answer is simple: *LOVE*! As hard as that may be for us to comprehend it must be so, it supports the idea that the angels were given free will and the power to choose. From that occurrence it reveals to us that the angels were not created and then forced to serve God, no they were not. No more than we are. Just like them, we were offered a choice!

So, you ask, where did lucifer come from and where did he get the idea to rebel against God? Well, you see God is love and true love will always allow a choice. True love allowed the angels to be "free moral agents" similar to what God has allowed mankind to be... And of course, as "free moral agents" lucifer and one-third of the angels chose to rebel. You see lucifer had [and still has] a false sense of his perceived greatness and feeling of equality with God... Now as "free moral agents" we know that we love God when we give up "our rights" back to Him.

Fallen angels:

We know that lucifer revolted against God, because he wanted to be like God and through his rebellion, he drew 1/3 of the angelic host in his rebellion. Here is what the Scripture say occurred after that rebellion:

Genesis 6:1-22
Now it came to pass, when men began to multiply on the face of the earth, and daughters were born to them, that the sons of God saw the daughters of men, that they were beautiful; and they took wives for themselves of all whom they chose. And the LORD said, "My Spirit shall not strive with man forever, for he is indeed flesh; yet his days shall be one hundred and twenty years." There were giants on the earth in those days, and also afterward, when the sons of God came in to the daughters of men and they bore children to them. Those were the mighty men who were of old, men of renown. Then the LORD saw that the wickedness of man was great in the earth, and that every intent of the thoughts of his heart was only evil continually. And the Lord was sorry that He had made man on the earth, and He was grieved in His heart. So the LORD said, "I will destroy man whom I have created from the face of the earth, both man and beast, creeping thing and birds of the air, for I am sorry that I have made them." But Noah found grace in the eyes of the LORD. This is the genealogy of Noah. Noah was a just man, perfect in his generations. Noah walked with God. And Noah begot three sons: Shem, Ham, and Japheth. The earth also was corrupt before God, and the earth was filled with violence. So God looked upon the earth, and indeed it was corrupt; for all flesh had corrupted their

way on the earth. And God said to Noah, "The end of all flesh has come before Me, for the earth is filled with violence through them; and behold, I will destroy them with the earth. Make yourself an ark of gopherwood; make rooms in the ark, and cover it inside and outside with pitch. And this is how you shall make it: The length of the ark shall be three hundred cubits, its width fifty cubits, and its height thirty cubits. You shall make a window for the ark, and you shall finish it to a cubit from above; and set the door of the ark in its side. You shall make it with lower, second, and third decks. And behold, I Myself am bringing floodwaters on the earth, to destroy from under heaven all flesh in which is the breath of life; everything that is on the earth shall die. But I will establish My covenant with you; and you shall go into the ark—you, your sons, your wife, and your sons' wives with you. And of every living thing of all flesh you shall bring two of every sort into the ark, to keep them alive with you; they shall be male and female. Of the birds after their kind, of animals after their kind, and of every creeping thing of the earth after its kind, two of every kind will come to you to keep them alive. And you shall take for yourself of all food that is eaten, and you shall gather it to yourself; and it shall be food for you and for them." Thus Noah did; according to all that God commanded him, so he did.

Here we read fallen angels having sexual relations with humans and producing hybrid offspring who would rule the world and further strengthen the systems of this world.

God began His search for someone who would be used to dismantle the systems of the world and bring them back to Him.

The creation of angels in the realm of eternity, with free will as God tested them. lucifer failed that test along with 1/3 of the heavenly host. They were banished to earth and Adam the first "God-man" was designed to be able to deal with them, but he also failed. And from that point began what we could call the systems of this world. It was at this point; I believe we began to witness God's Divine Council coming to bear in the affairs of mankind.

We would next explore the creation of man.

Let's check our understanding of the chapter "Creation of Angels."

1. What does it mean when you say that God is "Eternal"?

2. How will you explain God type 'agape' love?

3. What could have caused God to allow lucifer to convince one-third of the angels to him in rebellion against Him?

4. Jesus willingly submitted His will to that of His Fathers as Scripture records. How are we expected to show our love towards God?

5. What was the reason for lucifer to revolt against God and to drag 1/3 of the angelic host along with him?

CHAPTER SIX
THE CREATION OF MAN

THE CREATION OF ADAM THE FIRST MAN THAT HAD BOTH THE HEAVENLY AND earthly in him, when God breathed into him a divine body of revelation so that he did not have to be subjected to any form of training or learning but instinctively knew. Because we all know that the first man, Adam never had to be subjected to any form of learning as we do today. No, He was given a body of knowledge in that breath from the Spirit of God and instinctively just knew. He became God-like in his abilities. And in that act, I believe that God had made man **vice regent** [a person who rules or reigns: **A GOVERNOR**] with Him. Adam's main task was to govern the earth as a territory of Heaven. And we all know that he failed miserably in that undertaking. That when lucifer and his angels were cast down to the earth realm as part punishment for rebelling against their Creator, God Almighty, that they set out to corrupt man, thereby allowing them to lose that responsibility and for them to assume the rulership of the earth and to enforce their incorrect understanding of heavenly rule. After all, lucifer wanted to be like God; but we all know that he just could not and would never be able to. He has been completely defeated by the King of kings and Lord of lords, King Jesus.

With the fall of Adam and Eve, we saw lucifer take charge and ruled the earth. Here is what was said in Genesis 6:6-8

Then the Lᴏʀᴅ saw that the wickedness of man was great in the earth, and that every intent of the thoughts of his heart was only evil continually. And the Lord was sorry that He had made man on the earth, and He was grieved in His heart. So the Lᴏʀᴅ said, "I will destroy man whom I have created from the face of the earth, both man and beast, creeping thing and birds of the air, for I am sorry that I have made them." But Noah found grace in the eyes of the Lᴏʀᴅ.

In steps, Noah as the only man who found grace and favour in God's eyes and as such the entire planet was wiped out apart from Noah and his family—eight souls. They were used to establish a new breed upon the earth. The cosmic battle has been waging for this planet from the day Adam and Eve sinned and lucifer gained control of the planet.

God worked through Noah and several others, such as Abraham in whom He set up the whole aspect of Faith. He then decided to set up a nation, Israel who would serve Him and that He could have been married to. From this setup we had what we know as the Old Covenant System, which we would briefly look at next.

One thing that we understand about Abraham, is that he became the man of Faith that we were to all follow. Even before the establishment of the Old Covenant System under the Israelites God patterned His entire system of Faith, Tithing, and Salvation through this Patriarch. The New Testament Saints are known as sons of Abraham. He became the point of reference to what needed to be accomplished through Jesus Christ!

Galatians 3:7 reveals this to us:

Therefore know that only those who are of faith are sons of Abraham.

Galatians 3:27-29
For as many of you as were baptized into Christ have put on Christ. There is neither Jew nor Greek, there is neither slave nor free, there is neither male nor female; for you are all one in Christ Jesus. And if you are Christ's, then you are Abraham's seed, and heirs according to the promise.

Ok, so let us now take a look at the Old Covenant System.

Let's check our understanding of the chapter "Creation of Man."

1. How did God equip man with both Heavenly and earthly at the very creation?

2. What was he able to accomplish/access as a result of this duality?

3. How did man [Adam] lose his God given responsibility of governing the Earth as a territory of Heaven?

4. Who stepped into this void as governor/ruler of the Earth?

5. What did God have to say about the state of the Earth during that period of governance?

6. Why did God choose Noah and His family to establish a new breed upon the earth?

7. What is it about Abraham's life that God want's all of us to follow?

8. What is the entire Old Covenant system patterned after?

9. Why then are we, New Covenant Saints, called children of Abraham?

10. What connection does Abraham have, to what was to be accomplished through Jesus?

CHAPTER SEVEN
THE OLD COVENANT

THE OLD COVENANT/TESTAMENT WAS SET UP AS THE RECORD OF GOD'S DEALINGS with mankind as He continued His search for the ultimate man to deal with and dismantle satan's throne and rule upon this planet.

Finally, God decided to reveal a nation and that nation was Israel. Through the nation of Israel, He begins to set the stage for His ultimate plan. As we read through the Prophet Daniel about the coming of His Kingdom into the earth as a small stone that had the capacity and the power to dismantle and destroy this system that had been setup by lucifer, in the coming of His Only Son Jesus the Christ.

This is how God chose to reveal the coming of His Kingdom into the earth. He used a heathen king's dream to speak, which we would be dealing with in our next chapter.

Through the nation of Israel, He established the Old Covenant System of rules and laws to govern mankind. However, we do know that, that system failed as Israel continued to sin and be disobedient to their Lord and King. So He decided to come in the Person of His son, Jesus Christ to fulfill His ultimate plan.

However, before His Son's arrival we had a major prophetic interpretation through Daniel, who was used to interpret king Nebuchadnezzar's dream, which we would be looking at in our next chapter.

CHAPTER EIGHT
INTERPRETATION OF
KING NEBUCHADNEZZAR'S DREAM

Now, what king Nebuchadnezzar dreamt, and Daniel interpreted, was not just revelation to be written in a book, but that it was actually something that needed to be accomplished in the earth.

So, as one reads through the Book of Daniel one cannot help but notice/realize that it was in this Book we came to understand for the very first time the Kingdom of God coming into the earth. At that time Babylon was the strongest kingdom that ever existed. Babylon was stronger than Egypt. It was an impressive kingdom, and it was at the time of its existence that God chose to introduce the idea and revelation of His Kingdom and His being much more superior than Babylon and every other kingdom after.

King Nebuchadnezzar had this dream that troubles him, but he just cannot remember the dream. He calls for all the wise men in his kingdom. His thought was that he would get them to work their magic and be able to get the dream that he had and its interpretation. Of course no one could have revealed such to him. Of course, God was behind all of this because He wanted to reveal His servant Daniel to the king in a completely different way.

So it was under the reign of king Nebuchadnezzar of Babylon that the God of Heaven, decided to introduce the reality of His Kingdom coming into the earth. He gave him a dream that set things into motion. Let's explore that dream and its interpretation: Daniel 2:1-3

Now in the second year of Nebuchadnezzar's reign, Nebuchadnezzar had dreams; and his spirit was so troubled that his sleep left him. Then the king gave the command to call the magicians, the astrologers, the sorcerers, and the Chaldeans to tell the king his dreams. So they came and stood before the king. And the king said to them, "I have had a dream, and my spirit is anxious to know the dream."

This was not a normal dream therefore king Nebuchadnezzar was so troubled. The dynamic thing about this dream is that he insisted on an interpretation of the dream. Of course none of his magicians, astrologers, sorcerers or Chaldeans could tell the king what his dream was, much rather give its interpretation. It was at that point the God of Heaven caused Daniel to be brought to the forefront. He was given both the dream and its interpretation as he called upon the God of Heaven.

Magicians: stylist, scribe, engraver.

Astrologers: a quiver—that which holds the arrow, pointed the lines, gave direction to the people.

Sorcerers: A primitive root—to whisper a spell, i.e. To enchant or practise magic, witchcraft.

Chaldeans: a clod breaker—wisest in the land.

All these men practiced gazing illegally into the future, they were not schooled in the wisdom of God—they were the Babylonian prophets. In this instant they could not interpret because this Kairos was fixed to a source. When Babylon failed—Daniel was switched on. Daniel stepped outside of his own natural wisdom and experience, and drew from the Resource of God's Holy Spirit, and he got the answers.

Daniel 2:31-35—The Dream

*You, O king, were looking and behold, there was **a single great statue; that statue,** which was large and of extraordinary splendour, was standing in front of you, and its appearance was awesome. The head of that statue was made of fine gold, its breast and its arms of silver, its belly and its thighs of bronze, its legs of iron, its feet partly of iron and partly of clay. You continued looking until **a***

stone was cut out without hands, and it struck the statue on its feet *of iron and clay and crushed them. Then the iron, the clay, the bronze, the silver and the gold were crushed all at the same time and became like chaff from the summer threshing floors; and the wind carried them away so that not a trace of them was found. But the stone that struck the statue became* **a great mountain** *and filled the whole earth.* [Emphasis Author's]

Daniel 2:36-45 —The Interpretation
This was the dream; now we will tell its interpretation before the king. You, O king, are the king of kings, to whom the God of heaven has given the kingdom, the power, the strength and the glory; and wherever the sons of men dwell, or the beasts of the field, or the birds of the sky, He has given them into your hand and has caused you to rule over them all. You are the head of gold. After you there will arise another kingdom inferior to you, then another third kingdom of bronze, which will rule over all the earth. Then there will be a fourth kingdom as strong as iron; inasmuch as iron crushes and shatters all things, so, like iron that breaks in pieces, it will crush and break all these in pieces. In that you saw the feet and toes, partly of potter's clay and partly of iron, it will be a divided kingdom; but it will have in it the toughness of iron, inasmuch as you saw the iron mixed with common clay. As the toes of the feet were partly of iron and partly of pottery, so some of the kingdom will be strong and part of it will be brittle. And in that you saw the iron mixed with common clay, **they will combine with one another in the seed of men; but they will not adhere to one another,** *even as iron does not combine with pottery. In the days of those kings the God of heaven will set up a kingdom which will never be destroyed, and that kingdom will not be left for another people; it will crush and put an end to all these kingdoms, but it will itself endure forever. Inasmuch as you saw that a stone was cut out of the mountain without hands and that it crushed the iron, the bronze, the clay, the silver and the gold, the great God has made known to the king what will take place in the future; so the dream is true and its interpretation is trustworthy.* [Emphasis Author's]

Daniel's interpretation of the dream reveals some very powerful stuff that gave some incredible foresight about what we have already lived through. It was so accurate in its unfolding that there are some people who cannot believe that the Book of Daniel was written many Centuries before these events actually occurred. It also gives some much-needed clarity on what many are declaring today as being futuristic. It is worth the study.

One of the certain themes of the interpretation of the king's dream was the reality of the colliding of world systems. The kingdoms of the world against The Kingdom of God. In the interpretation there are several words and phrases that give incredible light and understanding as to how the Kingdom of God operates against the kingdoms of this world. They also reveal the structure and inner workings of the kingdoms of this world. Let's take the journey and explore them.

The first thing we see in the dream is that there was an impressive statue; "single great statue".

The Hebrew word used to describe great in what king Nebuchadnezzar saw is not the same as the word for great used in Verse 35, which we will get to next. The word used here to describe the greatness of the statue that he saw is "saggiy", meaning large in size and number but not great in terms of quality.

For example, it is similar to the statue of Buddha that one may see in many places; it looks large and great in size, but it is hollow on the inside. It has no substance! It only makes an impression, but once confronted its true quality is then revealed—this is what the Kingdom will confront.

This must be seen as the worldly system that wants to come into The Church—paying attention to external and does not focus on the internal. It is constantly diminishing in value; it is constantly going downwards. To the natural eye it may appear magnificent, but it diminishes in value and quality.

"Became a great mountain": The Hebrew word here for "great" is different to the one used earlier to describe the statue with the head of gold, etc. The word used here is the Hebrew "rab" meaning: superior, rank, internal capacity, describes leadership, also means to stand at the top.

After Daniel spent a considerable amount of time explaining the grandeur of the statue, he then compares it to a mountain. The stone representing the Kingdom of God, unlike the image began small. However, even though it was small it was solid throughout. There was nothing hollow about it. It was acquired from a much greater, rock-solid mountain. God pays attention to substance on the inside and not external appeal. If one had to choose between these two, unless they had revelation from God, they would have most likely chosen that which had the external appeal.

This stone was taken out of the mountain but not cut out by any human hands and then it proceeded to strike the statue/image. The Kingdom of God impacted the image and brought it down.

Hear me; impact will always require contact. Every system in the earth that carries this image will be confronted. As a matter-of-fact God confronts this position first in our hearts, before He uses us to impact the systems of the earth. Here are some things that must be realized about The Kingdom of God from the interpretation of this dream:

- The Kingdom begins on the inside of us and does not operate in a vacuum outside.
- The Kingdom is highly confrontational—God and His Word will constantly confront you.
- The Kingdom is highly transformational. The rock struck and all entities [gold, silver, bronze, iron, and clay] crumbled at the same time —the character of these entities was transformed to husk.
- The Kingdom does not rely on human strength.
- The Kingdom demands that we constantly empty ourselves of our own strength and become dependent on God.
- The Kingdom will always prove itself to be superior to all world systems.

The image was destroyed by the Rock [Kingdom] and this Rock [Kingdom] grew and grew until it "filled the whole earth"—not just certain structures in the earth—all the earth.

I truly find it interesting that God did not give this revelation to some Pastor in The Church because the Kingdom is not limited to a Church. The Prophet Jeremiah was given a glimpse of The Kingdom of God invading every territory in the earth. Here is what he recorded in Jeremiah 31:31-40

Behold, the days are coming, says the Lord, when I will make a new covenant with the house of Israel and with the house of Judah—not according to the covenant that I made with their fathers in the day that I took them by the hand to lead them out of the land of Egypt, My covenant which they broke, though I was a husband to them, says the Lord. But this is the covenant that I will make with the house of Israel after those days, says the Lord: I will put My law in their minds, and write it on their hearts; and I will be their God, and they shall be My people. No more shall every man teach his neighbour, and every man his brother, saying, 'Know the Lord,' for they all shall know Me, from the least of them to the greatest of them, says the Lord. For I will forgive their iniquity, and their sin I will remember no more." Thus says the Lord, Who gives the sun for a light by day, The ordinances of the moon and the stars for a light by night, Who disturbs the sea, And its waves roar (The Lord of hosts is His name): "If those ordinances depart From before Me, says the Lord, Then the seed of Israel shall also cease From being a nation before Me forever." Thus says the Lord: "If heaven above can be measured, And the foundations of the earth searched out beneath, I will also cast off all the seed of Israel For all that they have done, says the Lord. "Behold, the days are coming, says the Lord, that the city shall be built for the Lord from the Tower of Hananel to the Corner Gate. The surveyor's line shall again extend straight forward over the hill Gareb; then it shall turn toward Goath. And the whole valley of the dead bodies and of the ashes, and all the fields as far as the Brook Kidron, to the corner of the Horse Gate toward the east, shall be holy to the Lord. It shall not be plucked up or thrown down anymore forever.

The Prophet Jeremiah was prophesying about the days in which we are now living. He was speaking about the New Covenant coming into effect. God placed in Jeremiah's heart the introduction of a reformation concept. Jeremiah was describing the expansion of God's territory in the earth, in the lives of men. He was describing a reformation time, a time when the whole structure was changing. He was seeing a time when the Laws of God were to be inscribed on the heart of man and not on tablets of stone. He was speaking of a time when God's rule and His Kingdom would be extended beyond the borders of Israel, beyond what was considered to be holy into areas that were considered to be unclean. The Kingdom indeed was going to fill all the earth.

We know this because he was describing areas that were well known for their uncleanness. All the territories were outside of their areas and were considered unclean. They must extend themselves to all these places because they are being reclaimed as holy to the Lord. He declared: Jeremiah 31:39-40

The surveyor's line shall again extend straight forward over the hill Gareb; then it shall turn toward Goath. And the whole valley of the dead bodies and of the ashes, and all the fields as far as the Brook Kidron, to the corner of the Horse Gate toward the east, shall be holy to the Lord. It shall not be plucked up or thrown down anymore forever.

Gareb was a place dedicated to lepers. Jewish mentality will tell you that you were never to touch a leper, or your priestly anointing will be interfered with. God is always going beyond religious thinking.

Goath referred to the men of eminence, prominence. It was describing an area dedicated to the rich Siserians who lived outside the walls. Religion will teach us not to touch business and politics—but here we see God is pushing us into Kingdom and not just Church. Kingdom has a natural expansion feature to it; it encompasses both the rich and the poor, the educated and the uneducated, people from all spheres of life.

Daniel continued in his interpretation of the king's dream and here is what he revealed about the image. Remember there were different elements of the image, the head of gold, the chest of silver, the legs of iron and the feet part iron and part clay. He also went on to show that they will combine but will not adhere to one another.

They will combine but will not adhere: The image appeared to be impregnable and united, but this was a false appearance. In fact they do not commit. They are joined but not in covenant. This is exactly what the systems of the world are today; they seem grand and great, but they are hollow!

We cannot afford to have that aspect or any other aspect of the image in The Church, because it seeks to neutralize the things of God in The Church. It must start on a personal level and then flow to others. All worldly empires are destined for destruction and failure. I believe that this image represented antichrist. Although the image was in the form of a man, it represented a system; so is the antichrist.

THE IMAGE ITSELF

Let's briefly look at what the image that Nebuchadnezzar saw represented. The Word of God and History have already revealed to us what each aspect of the image represented.

The head of gold was identified as Babylon. Babylon [confusion] is the engine room of the ungodly systems of the earth, which is still operational today.

Breast and arms of silver was identified as the succeeding kingdom, Medo-Persia. It was to be inferior to the preceding kingdom, as silver is inferior to gold. In what respect inferior? Not in power, for it was its conqueror. Not in extent, for Cyrus subdued all the East from the Aegean Sea to the River Indus, and thus erected the most extensive empire that up to that time had ever existed. But it was inferior in wealth, luxury, and magnificence. Viewed from a Scriptural standpoint, the principal event under the Babylonish empire was the captivity of the children of Israel; so the principal event under the Medo-Persian kingdom was the restoration of Israel to their own land. At the taking of Babylon, B.C.538, Cyrus, as an act of courtesy, assigned the first place in the kingdom to his uncle, Darius. But two years afterwards B.C. 536 Darius died; and in the same year also died Cambyses, king of Persia, Cyrus' father. By these events, Cyrus was left sole monarch of the whole empire. In this year, which closed Israel's seventy years of captivity, Cyrus issued his famous decree for the return of the Jews and the rebuilding of their temple. This was the first instalment of the great decree for the restoration and building again of Jerusalem [Ezra 6:14], which was completed in the seventh year of the reign of Artaxerxes, B.C.457

Belly and thighs of bronze was identified as the Grecian Empire: The metal continued to decrease in value, and can be interpreted to refer to the decline in authority in Greek Empire. Although Alexander the Great was an intrepid leader and a brilliant strategist, his sudden death plunged the empire he had created into chaos. Generals who had fought under Alexander at first cooperated with his successor, Perdiccas, in dividing up Alexander's Empire, but then assassinated him in 321 BC. There followed forty years of war between "The Successors" [Diadochi]. By circa 300, Alexander's former empire had stabilized primarily into the four kingdoms of Cassander, Lysimachus, Ptolemy, and Seleucus [see Kingdoms of the Diadochi, 281 BC].

Just as Babylon and Medo-Persia are identified by name in the visions of Daniel, so is Greece. The angel Gabriel specifically identified the kingdom of Greece as the "shaggy goat" [Daniel 8:21], the "male goat" with a conspicuous horn that came from the west [Daniel 8:5-6] and completely overpowered the two-horned ram [Daniel 8:7], identified as the kings of Media and Persia [Daniel 8:20]. The large, conspicuous horn [Daniel 8:5, 8] refers to none other than Alexander the Great, who conquered the then-known world. The fact that this horn was broken [Daniel 8:8, 22] signifies Alexander's sudden, premature death in 323 B.C. The four horns that sprang up in place of the large horn [Daniel 8:22] represent the four kingdoms of Cassander, Lysimachus, Ptolemy, and Seleucus, whose corporate presence significantly reduced the power of Alexander in his empire. Greece is the third kingdom, the thighs of bronze, identified in Nebuchadnezzar's vision [Daniel 2:32, 39].

Legs of iron was identified as Rome! Daniel described the lower extremities of the statue in Nebuchadnezzar's dream thus: "Its legs of iron, its feet partly of iron and partly of clay" [Daniel 2:33]. He also designated this description as referring to "a fourth kingdom" [Daniel 2:40]. This fourth kingdom is nowhere identified by name in the book of Daniel. Daniel stated, however, that "it" (the fourth kingdom) "will crush and break all these in pieces" [Daniel 2:40]. "All these" refers to the preceding third kingdom and any vestiges of the first and second kingdoms. Consequently, we believe we are justified in identifying this fourth kingdom as the Roman Empire. Also many Bible Scholars and Historians have come to the same conclusion.

The Roman Empire certainly displaced the Greek Empire [Daniel 8:21], as well as the Medo-Persian [Daniel 8:20] and Babylonian [Daniel 2:38] Empires, each of which *is* named in Daniel. This Roman Empire was represented by the two legs. This was further highlighted in the fact that the Roman Empire eventually divided into a Western [Roman] segment and an eastern [Byzantine] segment. Constantine the Great "is thought of as the founder of the Eastern Roman Empire." This event is symbolized by his building an imperial residence in Byzantium, which he renamed

Constantinople. Constantinople later became the capital of the Eastern Roman Empire.

Feet of iron and clay was identified as follows: By 324 AD Constantine was emperor over the ten territories of the entire Roman Empire, which are prophesied as, "The Ten Horns or Kingdoms of Daniel's Prophecy," and they were:

1. Spain [includes Portugal or Lusitania]
2. Gaul [France]
3. Germany
4. Britain
5. Italy
6. Rhaetia [Tyrol and Bavaria or portions of Switzerland and Austria]
7. North Africa
8. Pannoniae [portions of Hungary and Yugoslavia]
9. Moesia [Goth or Bulgaria in Asia Minor]
10. Thrace [Greece and Turkey in Asia Minor

The Arrival of The Kingdom of God: Daniel 2:43-46

And as the toes of the feet were partly of iron and partly of clay, so the kingdom shall be partly strong and partly fragile. As you saw iron mixed with ceramic clay, **they will mingle with the seed of men;** *but they will not adhere to one another, just as iron does not mix with clay.* **And in the days of these kings the God of heaven will set up a kingdom which shall never be destroyed; and the kingdom shall not be left to other people; it shall break in pieces and consume all these kingdoms, and it shall stand forever.** *Inasmuch as you saw that the stone was cut out of the mountain without hands, and that it broke in pieces the iron, the bronze, the clay, the silver, and the gold—the great God has made known to the king what will come to pass after this.* **The dream is certain, and its interpretation is sure.** [Emphasis Author's]

I believe that there are some very important statements in the above Passage of Scripture that I would like to randomly highlight.

In his interpretation Daniel made a very clear statement that cannot be misconstrued when he said: "In the days of these kings the God of Heaven will set up His Kingdom and it shall never be destroyed."

What this was telling us is this: The Kingdom of God will be in the earth when the image represented by the four kingdoms is already in the earth. It does not say that the destruction of the image represents the introduction of The Kingdom into the earth. No! In order for the destruction to take place the Kingdom had to be already in the earth. It had to have been already set up! In light of this understanding we could now understand that the arrival of the Kingdom and the destruction of the image are not one and the same event. I believe that the Kingdom fully arrived on the Day of Pentecost and has been active ever since. We shall discuss The Kingdom in a bit more detail in chapter ten of this book.

"The God of Heaven will *set up* His Kingdom." *Set up* comes from the Hebrew quwm and is rendered: to be securely position, established, and divinely arranged.

This, therefore, lends to the idea that one cannot subscribe to the Kingdom of God and still live lawlessly. The Kingdom is divinely arranged, and it is securely established. In essence it functions by Divine laws, and it is well ordered. So as Kingdom Citizens we must submit to the laws of The Kingdom.

Remember that the Kingdom in this instance is represented by a stone cut out of a mountain, it was solid throughout. Unlike the image that was massive and grand but hollow on the inside. The Kingdom's emphasis is internal grandeur and not external appeal like the systems of the world.

Worldly systems depicted by the image can be described as a system that is antichrist in nature that seeks to imprison our souls and define our lives in opposition to divine standards. These systems will mock anything that does not conform to its code. The world is advanced and propelled by the flesh. The Kingdom of God is advanced by adhering to and living our lives by the laws and values of The Kingdom in the midst of decaying values of the world system.

Verse 43 reveals to us the primary communicator of the dynamics of the world systems: "In the seed of men": man; unregenerate man is the primary communicator. As such the systems of this world are constantly cascading downwards and diminishing. The Kingdom of God on the other hand, is constantly growing and not diminishing. Image/Statue is constantly moving to a place of weakness—starts with gold and diminishes to clay.

Converting the systems of this world to the Kingdom of God is a long and difficult process, but one that MUST be DONE! For that we need a new breed of Christians who would take this word to heart and lay the groundwork for those following, just as Jesus and His early Apostles did. We need to have a group of Saints that will not buy into the established traditions and continue to "toe the line" but who would break with tradition and see God manifest on their behalf in powerful ways.

We cannot afford to continue with the "business as usual" mantra but seek to bring true and substantial change to the governing systems of the world. And in doing so, that we would not just seek government's approval for everything that we have been Divinely called to accomplish. That we need those who would support a move of God that would not bow to the system's "Charity Status" but who will press on without any of that stuff if need be.

Let's check our understanding of the chapter "Interpretation of King Nebuchadnezzar's Dream."

1. What was the reason that the magicians, astrologers, sorcerers, and the Chaldeans of King Nebuchadnezzar's Day unable to offer an interpretation of his dream?

2. Could it be possible that God orchestrated these events so that His Prophet Daniel could be brought to the forefront?

3. When did Daniel receive the dream and its interpretation from God?

4. What was one of the obvious themes of the interpretation of King Nebuchadnezzar's dream?

5. What was the Hebrew word translated "great" in Daniel 2:31 to describe the greatness of the statue that King Nebuchadnezzar saw in his dream? What does it mean?

6. What is the Hebrew word translated "great" in Daniel 2:35 describing the mountain into which the stone grew?

7. What is represented by the stone cut out without hands which struck the "great statue"?

8. According to Daniel, how was the Kingdom of God expected begin and expand upon the earth?

9. What are the 6 things that we need to understand about the Kingdom of God from the interpretation of this dream?

10. How do you understand/explain Jeremiah 31:31-40?

11. What is revealed by the different parts of the image being made of different material?

12. Explain what each part of the great image represented?

13. What was Daniel 8:8,22 predicting, would occur in the future?

14. Do you agree that the 4ᵗʰ Kingdom spoken of by Daniel is the Roman Empire? Why or why not?

15. Who are the 10 nations described by Daniel as 10 horns in his prophesy?

16. According to Daniel's interpretation of the dream, during which time was the God of Heaven to setup His Kingdom?

17. What is the Hebrew word translated "setup" in Daniel 2:44? What does it mean?

18. How will you contrast the systems of the world against the systems of the Kingdom of God?

CHAPTER NINE
JESUS THE SECOND MAN AND LAST ADAM

<small>After the fall of the first man Adam, everyone that was born was born</small> after the fallen Adam and the human race continued in that vein until the appearance of Jesus Christ. He was not born of the seed of Adam, but Mary was impregnated via the Holy Spirit. That Jesus would be the Second Man designed to bring an end to all satanic rule. He was going to be born of the Holy Spirit, just like Adam was before he fell through the temptation of the devil. However, Jesus, as you know, did not cave into the temptations of the devil.

1 Corinthians 15:45-49
And so it is written, "The first man Adam became a living being." The last Adam became a life-giving spirit. However, the spiritual is not first, but the natural, and afterward the spiritual. The first man was of the earth, made of dust; the second Man is the Lord from heaven. As was the man of dust, so also are those who are made of dust; and as is the heavenly Man, so also are those who are heavenly. And as we have borne the image of the man of dust, we shall also bear the image of the heavenly Man.

Jesus not only lived the perfect life, but He willingly paid the price so that all of humanity could be redeemed, by going to the Cross and die and being raised again from the dead to become the first in a new species, which would later be used to totally dismantle the systems of this world.

We are currently seeing the Kingdom of God being advanced and strengthened in the earth and this will continue until ALL the kingdoms of this world become the kingdoms of our Lord and where Jesus is rightfully reigning forevermore.

We know that with Jesus' arrival on planet earth the King of the Kingdom and the Kingdom itself arrived. His preaching and teaching was all about the Kingdom of God. It was not until He knew that His time to exit His life upon earth that He revealed that He would be establishing an entity called the Church [or Ecclesia] to train Christians in the ways of the Kingdom of God.

However, there is something that I discovered as I read Jesus' parables of the Kingdom that I would like to present to you. Here it is:

There are 14 parables concerning the Kingdom [there are also 18 others recorded in Scripture, but they were not on the Kingdom] and I will like for us to look at the first parable Jesus spoke about the Kingdom. As a matter He revealed that if we do not understand this first Parable, we won't be able to understand any of the other Parables. Let me just list the 14. In this writing we would be looking at the first.

1. **The Sower and the Seed**—Matthew 13:1-23, 36-43
2. **The Wheat and the Tares**—Matthew 13:24-30
3. **The Grain of Mustard Seed**—Matthew 13:31-32
4. **The Leaven**—Matthew 13:33-35
5. **The Hidden Treasure**—Matthew 13:44
6. **The Pearl of Great Price**—Matthew 13:45-46
7. **The Net Cast into the Sea**—Matthew 13:47-50
8. **The Householder**—Matthew 13:51-53
9. **The Unmerciful King's Servants**—Matthew 18:23-35
10. **The Labourers in the Vineyard**—Matthew 20:1-16
11. **The Marriage Feast**—Matthew 22:1-14
12. **The Ten Virgins**—Matthew 25:1-13
13. **The Talents**—Matthew 25:14-30
14. **The Growing Seed**—Mark 4:26-29

1ᵀ PARABLE: THE SOWER AND THE SEED MATTHEW 13:1-23

*On the same day Jesus went out of the house and sat by the sea. And great multitudes were gathered together to Him, so that He got into a boat and sat; and the whole multitude stood on the shore. Then He spoke many things to them in parables, saying: "Behold, a sower went out to sow. And as he sowed, some **seed** fell by the wayside; and the birds came and devoured them. Some fell on stony places, where they did not have much earth; and they immediately sprang up because they had no depth of earth. But when the sun was up they were scorched, and because they had no root they withered away. And some fell among thorns, and the thorns sprang up and choked them. But others fell on good ground and yielded a crop: some a hundredfold, some sixty, some thirty. He who has ears to hear, let him hear!" And the disciples came and said to Him, "Why do You speak to them in parables?" He answered and said to them, "Because it has been given to you to know the mysteries of the kingdom of heaven, but to them it has not been given. For whoever has, to him more will be given, and he will have abundance; but whoever does not have, even what he has will be taken away from him. Therefore I speak to them in parables, because seeing they do not see, and hearing they do not hear, nor do they understand. And in them the prophecy of Isaiah is fulfilled, which says: 'Hearing you will hear and shall not understand, And seeing you will see and not perceive; For the hearts of this people have grown dull. Their ears are hard of hearing, And their eyes they have closed, Lest they should see with their eyes and hear with their ears, Lest they should understand with their hearts and turn, So that I should heal them.' But blessed are your eyes for they see, and your ears for they hear; for assuredly, I say to you that many prophets and righteous men desired to see what you see, and did not see it, and to hear what you hear, and did not hear it. "Therefore hear the parable of the sower: When anyone hears the word of the kingdom, and does not understand it, then the wicked one comes and snatches away what was sown in his heart. This is he who received seed by the wayside. But he who received the seed on stony places, this is he who hears the word and immediately receives it with joy; yet he has no root in* *himself, but endures only for a while. For when tribulation or per-secution arises because of the word, immediately he stumbles. Now he who received seed among the thorns is he who hears the word, and the cares of this world and the deceitfulness of riches choke the word, and he becomes unfruitful. But he who received seed on the good ground is he who hears the word and understands it, who indeed bears fruit and produces: some a hundredfold, some sixty, some thirty.*

[Jesus was teaching concerning the mysteries of the Kingdom] – Matthew 13:1-23, 36-43 Matthew, Mark 4:3-9 and Luke 8:4-8 all recorded this Parable – This was the very first Parable that Jesus spoke and as such it is vital that we understand it as it would set the tone for all others. As a matter-of-fact Mark recorded this in Mark 4:13:

And He said to them, Do you not know this parable? And how then will you know all parables?

It is one of the few parables in which we actually have Jesus' own interpretation of the parable.

The value of this parable becomes clearer in the light of Jesus' explanation, for by it we can see ourselves as we really are in regard to how we have received the Word into our lives...

EXPLANATION OF THE PARABLE
A. "The Sower."

Who is the Sower? – Not specifically mentioned, but let us look at Matthew 13:37

This is in explanation of "The Parable Of The Wheat And The Tares"—In which Jesus explains "**He who sows the good seed is the Son of Man.**"

Something about the seed that I would like for us to understand; and it is as follows: when a seed is planted in the soil and it first dies and is then resurrected, it breaks through the soil. In doing so it demonstrates a Kingdom mentality as it grows against gravity, which pulls everything down to earth. The seed grows towards the sun. In like manner, we as Kingdom Saints, we also grow against the gravitational pull of this world system. We grow towards THE SON—Jesus, the Christ!

So it is likely that the "Sower" in this parable had immediate reference to Jesus. But **it is a fair use** of the parable to apply it today to anyone who faithfully proclaims the message of the Son of Man, which is the Gospel of The Kingdom

B. "The Seed".
1. The seed is "the word of the Kingdom"—Matthew 13:19a—**When anyone hears the word of the Kingdom, and does not understand *it*,**
2. The gospel of the Kingdom, which was the theme of Jesus' preaching—Matthew 4:23—**And Jesus went about all Galilee, teaching in their synagogues, preaching the gospel of the Kingdom, and healing all kinds of sickness and all kinds of disease among the people.**
3. It was also an important element of apostolic preaching—Acts 8:12; 28:30-31—**But when they believed Philip as he preached the things concerning the Kingdom of God and the name of Jesus Christ, both men and women were baptized.**

   Then Paul dwelt two whole years in his own rented house, and received all who came to him, preaching the Kingdom of God and teaching the things which concern the Lord Jesus Christ with all confidence, no one forbidding him.

C. "The Wayside" [The First Soil].
This soil represents one who "hears...and does not understand"—Matthew 13:19a

Most likely, these are those who have hardened their hearts prior to hearing the Word—Matthew 13:10-15

And the disciples came and said to Him, "Why do You speak to them in parables?" He answered and said to them, "Because it has been given to you to know the mysteries of the kingdom of heaven, but to them it has not been given. For whoever has, to him more will be given, and he will have abundance; but whoever does not have, even what he has will be taken away from him. Therefore I speak to them in parables, because seeing they do not see, and hearing they do not hear, nor do they understand. And in them the prophecy of Isaiah is fulfilled, which says 'Hearing you will hear and shall not understand, And seeing you will see and not perceive; For the hearts of this people have grown dull. Their ears are hard of hearing, And their eyes they have closed, Lest they should see with their eyes and hear with their ears, Lest they should understand with their hearts and turn, So that I should heal them.'

The "birds" represent "the wicked one" [called "the devil" in Luke 8:12]

- Who snatches away the Word from those whose hearts are hardened.
- Their condition therefore is one of being "blinded" by the evil one to the Gospel—2 Corinthians 4:3-4

But even if our gospel is veiled, it is veiled to those who are perishing, whose minds the god of this age has blinded, who do not believe, lest the light of the gospel of the glory of Christ, who is the image of God, should shine on them.

- While satan contributes to their blindness, it is precipitated by their own hardness of heart!

D. "The Stony Places" [The Second Soil].
This soil represents the one who...

- "hears the word and immediately receives it with joy"—Matthew 13:20
- "yet he has no root in himself, but endures only for a while"—Matthew 13:21a
- "when tribulation or persecution arises because of the word, immediately he stumbles"—Matthew 13:21b.
- Some hear the Word and receive it with great joy.
- But with no root, they are not grounded in the Word.
- So that when troubles arise, there is no endurance and stumbling occurs.
- Here we learn that an emotional reception **without** a strong foundation based upon the Word will not enable one to stand against tribulation and persecution.

E. "Among The Thorns" [The Third Soil].

This soil represents the one who.

- "hears the word"—Matthew 13:22a—Now he who received seed among the thorns is he who hears the word.
- But whose ability to bear fruit is choked by:
  1) "the cares of this world"—Matthew 13:22b
  2) "the deceitfulness of riches"—Matthew 13:22c
  3) "pleasures of life" [added in Luke 8:14—Now the ones *that* fell among thorns are those who, when they have heard, go out and are choked with cares, riches, and pleasures of life, and bring no fruit to maturity.]

How these three "thorns" can cause us to be unfruitful is explained in other portions of God's Word.

a. The cares of this world
1. Can cause us to be unprepared – for example - Luke 21:34-36 [**ISV**]

Constantly be on your guard so that your hearts may not be loaded down with self-indulgence, drunkenness, and the worries of this life, or that day will take you by surprise like a trap. For it will come on all who live on the face of the earth. So be alert at all times, praying that you may have strength to escape all these things that are going to take place and to take your stand in the presence of the Son of Man.

2. The evil in cares and anxieties is that they can detract our minds from what is truly important—Luke 12:29-32

So stop concerning yourselves about what you will eat or what you will drink, and stop being distressed. For it is the gentiles who are concerned about all these things. Surely your Father knows that you need them! Instead, be concerned about his kingdom, and these things will be provided for you as well. Stop being afraid, little flock, for your Father is pleased to give you the kingdom.

b. The deceitfulness of riches
   1. The danger is described in 1 Timothy 6:9-10

But people who want to get rich keep toppling into temptation and are trapped by many stupid and harmful desires that plunge them into destruction and ruin. For the love of money is a root of all kinds of evil. Some people, in their eagerness to get rich, have wandered away from the faith and pierced themselves with much pain.

   2. Again, the evil in riches lay in diverting our attention away from God, and feeling self-sufficient—1 Timothy 6:17

Tell those who are rich in the present world not to be arrogant and not to place their confidence in anything as uncertain as riches. Instead, let them place their confidence in God, who lavishly provides us with everything for our enjoyment.

c. Pleasures of life
   1. Those involving the flesh in particular divert our minds from the things of the Spirit—Galatians 5:17

For what the flesh wants is opposed to the Spirit, and what the Spirit wants is opposed to the flesh. They are opposed to each other, and so you do not do what you want to do.

   2. Sowing to the flesh make it **impossible** to reap of the Spirit!—Galatians 6:7-9

Stop being deceived; God is not to be ridiculed. A person harvests whatever he plants. For the person who plants in his flesh will harvest decay from the flesh, but the person who plants in the Spirit will harvest eternal life from the Spirit. Let us not get tired of doing what is good, for at the right time we will reap a harvest-if we do not give up. **This is so important. We need to be constantly aware of this in the world system we are functioning in! God sees.**

F. "The Good Ground" [The Fourth Soil].

- This soil represents the one who.
- "hears the word and understands it"—Matthew 13:23a.
- "indeed bears fruit and produces"—Matthew 13:23b.
- Luke adds that he hears "the word with a noble and good heart", and then "keeps it and bears fruit with patience"—Luke 8:15.

Those with "a noble and good heart", they, are the ones.
- Who will understand the Word.
- Who will keep it, and with patience produce fruit in their lives!
- They will be like the Bereans, who were commended for being "fair-minded", as manifested in the way they:
- "received the word will all readiness."
- "searched the Scriptures daily to find out whether these things were so"—Acts 17:11

Note the importance of "understanding" in relation to "bearing fruit".
- Jesus made the connection between the two in this parable—Matthew 13:23

    "But as for what was sown on good soil, this is the person who **hears** the word, **understands** it, and **produces** a crop that yields a hundred, sixty, or thirty times what was sown."
- Paul connects the two when he writes of the gospel producing fruit among the Colossians "since the day they heard [NASV says "understood"] the grace of God in truth"—Colossians 1:5-6

because of the hope reserved for you in heaven, of which you previously heard in the word of truth, the gospel which has come to you, just as in all the world also it is bearing fruit and increasing, even as it has been doing in you also since the day you heard it and under-stood the grace of God in truth;

- When one "understands", they will more likely "bear fruit"; but the key to understanding is having a "good and noble heart" that is willing to listen and learn!

And what kinds of "fruit" will one bear? There are different kinds.

1. The fruit of winning souls to Christ—Romans 1:13
2. The fruit of practical holiness—Romans 6:22
3. The fruit of the Spirit [i.e., a Christ-like character]—Galatians 5:22-23
4. The fruit of good works—Colossians 1:10
5. The fruit of praise & thanksgiving—Hebrews 13:15

An important observation is that not all will bear the same amount.

1. "some a hundredfold, some sixty, some thirty"—Matthew 13:23
2. As illustrated in The Parable of the Talents, some may be given more according to their ability to use what God has given them—Matthew 25:14-15
3. Whatever our ability, we should exercise it accordingly—1 Peter 4:10-11—"As good managers of God's grace in its various forms, serve one another with the gift each of you has received. Whoever speaks must speak God's words. Whoever serves must serve with the strength that God supplies, so that in every way God may be glorified through Jesus Christ. Glory and power belong to him forever and ever! Amen."

With the explanation provided by Jesus Himself, we should have little problem understanding The Parable of The Sower and the spiritual truths Jesus was teaching.

However, it is **one thing to understand it, quite another to make application of** it. Seeking to make application in a thought-provoking way, let me ask "What kind of soil are you?"

WHAT IS THE APPLICATION OF THE PARABLE?

A. Are You Like "The Wayside"?

1. If you have heard the gospel of Christ and His Kingdom, but are not yet a Christian!
2. You may be in the process of hardening your heart the longer you wait!

3. You are susceptible to demonic deception in some form, to blind you and not allow the Word of God to have its intended effect!

B. Are You Like "The Stony Places"?

1. If you responded to the Gospel at one time, but are not being grounded in the faith!
2. You will likely fall away when persecution or temptation comes your way!

C. Are You Like The Soil "Among The Thorns"?

1. If you responded to the gospel at one time, but are becoming too preoccupied with the cares, riches, and pleasures of this world!
2. You will not be able to bear much fruit!—And remember what Jesus said about branches that don't bear fruit!—John 15:1-6

D. Are You Like "The Good Soil"?

1. If you have responded to the Gospel of the Kingdom, and are bearing fruit!
2. Then you have demonstrated several important things:
   • You have a good and noble heart!
   • You have come to understand the Word!
   • You have been keeping it with patience!
3. And so the Word of God has been able to produce its intended effect in you!

Once we get this Parable, then we are able to both understand all the other Parables of the Kingdom and we become able to release a full understanding of the Kingdom to others.

In our next chapter, we would be taking a look at the Kingdom of God and the New Covenant.

Let's check our understanding of the chapter "Jesus the Second Man and the Last Adam."

1. Do you agree that while there are differences between the births of Adam (First) and Jesus Christ (Last Adam) based on Scripture?
2. What gives you the confidence that as a human your spirit bears the image of God?

3. Which Scriptures speak to the fact that Jesus willingly paid the price for the sins of all humanity?
4. The author states "we are currently seeing the Kingdom of God being advanced and strengthened in the earth". What are your views on this?
5. What is the purpose of the Church or "Ecclesia"?
6. How many of the parables recorded in the New Testament are about the Kingdom of God?
7. Which is the first parable Jesus spoke about the Kingdom of God?
8. Why is it necessary for us to fully understand this first parable Jesus spoke about the Kingdom?
9. Match the descriptions in Column A below with it's matching persona in Column B

COLUMN A	COLUMN B
He who Sows the Good Seed	The Seed
The word of the Kingdom	Son of Man
The ones who "hears... and does not understand"	The Birds
Those who immediately receives the word with Joy but lack a strong foundation and therefore unable to stand against tribulation/persecution.	The Way Side
Who snatches away the Word from those whose hearts are hardened.	The Stony Places
Those who have hardened their hearts thereby allowing satan to snatch the good seed.	The Good Ground
Those who hears the word and their ability to bear fruit is choked.	The Ones who are "Blinded"
Those with "a noble and good heart"	The Thorns

10. Explain using Scripture, how these three types of "thorns" can cause us to be unfruitful:

    a) the "cares of this world" (Matthew 13:22b)

    b) the "deceitfulness of riches" (Matthew 13:22c)

    c) the "pleasures of life" (Luke 8:14)

11. What is the importance of "understanding" in relation to "bearing fruit"?

12. Based on Scripture, what types of "fruit" are we to bear?

13. How is it possible that not all "seed" falling on "good ground" will not produce the same amount of harvest.

14. If you were to apply this to yourself ... what kind of soil would you consider yourself to be?

15. What are the two main benefits of understanding this parable?

CHAPTER TEN
THE KINGDOM OF GOD
AND THE NEW COVENANT

Finally, the 4000-year wait was over from the fall of Adam and Eve, God had been establishing a lineage for His Son to arrive on the planet!

He could not have come before, because 'the fullness of time' had not yet come. In the book of Daniel, we read about Babylon one of the greatest empires that ever existed and the dream that Daniel had to interpret and for the first time we see plainly the mention of The Kingdom of God manifesting in the earth.

[4]The book of Daniel records some of the most accurate and powerful truths concerning the Kingdom of God. God gave king Nebuchadnezzar a dream, which he could not recall. Here is what the first 12 verses of Daniel chapter 2 states:

Now in the second year of Nebuchadnezzar's reign, Nebuchadnezzar had dreams; and his spirit was so troubled that his sleep left him. Then the king gave the command to call the magicians, the astrologers, the sorcerers, and the Chaldeans to tell the king his dreams. So they came and stood before the king. And the king said to them, "I have had a dream, and my spirit is anxious to know the dream." Then the Chaldeans spoke to the king in Aramaic, "O king,

---

[4] From the Author's book - Understanding the Kingdom of God and the Church of Jesus Christ. Can be sourced here: apostlemscantlebury.com

live forever! Tell your servants the dream, and we will give the in-terpretation." The king answered and said to the Chaldeans, "My decision is firm: if you do not make known the dream to me, and its interpretation, you shall be cut in pieces, and your houses shall be made an ash heap. However, if you tell the dream and its interpre-tation, you shall receive from me gifts, rewards, and great honor. Therefore tell me the dream and its interpretation." They answered again and said, "Let the king tell his servants the dream, and we will give its interpretation." The king answered and said, "I know for certain that you would gain time, because you see that my deci-sion is firm: if you do not make known the dream to me, there is only one decree for you! For you have agreed to speak lying and corrupt words before me till the time has changed. Therefore tell me the dream, and I shall know that you can give me its interpretation." The Chaldeans answered the king, and said, "There is not a man on earth who can tell the king's matter; therefore no king, lord, or rul-er has ever asked such things of any magician, astrologer, or Chal-dean. It is a difficult thing that the king requests, and there is no other who can tell it to the king except the gods, whose dwelling is not with flesh." For this reason the king was angry and very furious, and gave the command to destroy all the wise men of Babylon. So the decree went out, and they began killing the wise men; and they sought Daniel and his companions, to kill them.

In the rest of chapter two Daniel gives the interpretation of the dream. Daniel was declaring the colliding of world systems.

Verse 31 reveals a powerful truth. Here is what it says: *You, O king, were watching; and behold, a great image! This great image, whose splen-dor* was *excellent, stood before you; and its form* was *awesome.*

However, the NASB version of the Bible translates the great image more clearly and I would like for us to look at it from that translation.

NASB—"SINGLE GREAT STATUE" VERSE 31
The word used to describe great in what king Nebuchadnezzar saw is not the same as the word for great used in verse 35. Here is what verse 35 says,

Then the iron, the clay, the bronze, the silver and the gold were crushed all at the same time and became like chaff from the summer threshing floors; and the wind carried them away so that not a trace of them was found. But the stone that struck the statue be-came a great mountain and filled the whole earth. [Emphasis Author's] NASB

The word used to describe what Nebuchadnezzar saw is "**Saggiy**"—large in size and number but not great in terms of quality. Similar to the statue of Buddha—looks large in size but it is hollow on the inside. It has no substance—now this is what the Kingdom will confront.

This must be seen as the worldly system that wants to come into the Church—that which only pays attention to the external and does not focus on the internal. It is constantly diminishing in value; it is constantly going downwards. To the natural eye it may appear magnificent, but it diminishes in value and quality. Yes, it is like the statute that king Nebuchadnezzar saw, large but hollow internally, without substance!

Ok, so let us go back and read the build-up to this 'great' that Daniel was describing. Verses 31-35

You, O king, were looking and behold, there was a single great stat-ue; that statue, which was large and of extraordinary splendor, was standing in front of you, and its appearance was awesome. The head of that statue was made of fine gold, its breast and its arms of silver, its belly and its thighs of bronze, its legs of iron, its feet partly of iron and partly of clay. You continued looking until a stone was cut out without hands, and it struck the statue on its feet of iron and clay and crushed them. Then the iron, the clay, the bronze, the silver and the gold were crushed all at the same time and be-came like chaff from the summer threshing floors; and the wind carried them away so that not a trace of them was found. But the stone that struck the statue became a great mountain and filled the whole earth. NASB

You continued looking until a stone was cut out without hands—very important statement. This stone represents something of quality and of a valuable substance. This is what king Nebuchadnezzar's image would confront. From this we realize that an image without any substance or value would be confronted by a substance/image that had great value and quality. We will speak more about this a bit later on.

"Became A Great Mountain"—"great"—"rab"—superior, rank, internal capacity, describes leadership—to stand at the top. Daniel spent time explaining the grandeur of the statue and then compares it to a mountain. God pays attention to substance on the inside and not external appeal. If we had to choose between these two if we do not have revelation from God, we will choose that which has external appeal.

NOT CUT OUT BY HUMAN HANDS AND STRUCK THE STATUE

Impact will always require contact. Every system that carries this image will be confronted God confronts this position in our hearts first. The Kingdom starts on the inside of us and does not operate in a vacuum outside. The Kingdom is highly confrontational—God and His Word will constantly confront you. The Kingdom is highly transformational. The rock struck and all entities [gold, silver, iron and clay] crumbled at the same time—the character of these entities was transformed to husk.

The Kingdom does not rely on human strength. The Kingdom demands that we constantly empty ourselves of our own strength and become dependent on God. The Kingdom will always prove itself to be superior to all world systems.

"Filled The Whole Earth"—not just certain structures in the earth—all the earth. *This Is Why Kingdom Cannot Be Contained In The Church: It Is Global In Every Respect.*

God did not give this revelation to some Pastor because the Kingdom is not limited to a Church. God is a God of Reformation, and His concept of Reformation goes far beyond mere religious thinking. The Book of Jeremiah gives us some insight that I would like for us to look at Jeremiah 31:38-40, which says:

> *Behold, the days are coming, says the Lord, that the city shall be built for the Lord from the Tower of Hananel to the Corner Gate. The surveyor's line shall again extend straight forward over the hill Gareb; then it shall turn toward Goath. And the whole valley of the dead bodies and of the ashes, and all the fields as far as the Brook Kidron, to the corner of the Horse Gate toward the east, shall be*

holy to the Lord. It shall not be plucked up or thrown down any-more forever.

Here Jeremiah was describing the expansion, the Lord was bringing—he was describing a reformation time, God was going to be dealing with man, and as such the whole structure was changing. All the territories were outside of their areas and were considered unclean. They must extend themselves to all these places because they are being reclaimed as holy to the Lord.

There are two regions spoken of here that we would do well to understand what they were.

One was **Gareb**—this was a place that was dedicated to lepers. It is from Hebrew *gaarab*, which carries the following meaning: "to scrape," Syriac, leprosy, the locality outside the city to which, lepers were removed, on the Northwest side of the city, West of the valley of Gihon.

Jewish mentality will tell you, never to touch or your priestly anointing is interfered with. God is always going beyond religious thinking.

The second is **Goath**—and this was a region that was dedicated to the men of eminence and prominence—describing an area dedicated to rich Siserians who lived outside the walls.

So now I would like you to grasp this; religion will teach us not to touch business and politics—but here we see God is pushing us into Kingdom and not just Church. Kingdom has a natural expansion feature to it—not limited to religious elements. Leaders must become more multifaceted—they cannot just be Bible school graduates. They must possess, and be skilled in the languages of the people as well as the language of the Lord.

Malachi 2:7 say, *For the lips of a priest should keep knowledge, And people should seek the law from his mouth; For he is the messenger of the Lord of hosts.* Now when people have a thirst for deeper things of God that the priests can no longer satisfy, it puts a demand on the priests to expand.

Verse 43 NASB reveals the following: **"They Will Combine but Will Not Adhere."**

This towering image appears to be impregnable and united, but this is a false appearance. They do not commit. They are joined but not in covenant. It seeks to neutralize the things of God in the earth—it is inside the Church. It must start on a personal level and then flow to others. Combine themselves together and express themselves in man. He saw an image of a man—self-indulgent. All worldly empires are destined for destruction and failure. [This is why anti-Christ is a system and not just a man; like this image being represented as a man yet it is a system so is the anti-Christ.]

Please understand this: The Kingdom of God is growing and not diminishing. Statue is constantly moving to a place of weakness—starts with gold and diminishes to clay. While the Kingdom began as a small stone [representing substance] cut out of the mountain began to grow and grow until it covered the entire earth. Showing us that the Kingdom began small but once it began there can be no stopping it, it will continue to grow and to increase!

This was not a normal dream therefore king Nebuchadnezzar was so troubled. The dynamic thing about this dream is that he insisted on an interpretation of the dream. So, he first turned to that which his system produced.

Magicians—stylist—scribe, engraver. Same word used in Hebrew Language—chisel—also chisel used to shape the cow.

Astrologers—a quiver—that which holds the arrow, pointed the lines, gave direction to the people.

Caldeans—a clod breaker—wisest in the land.

All these men practiced gazing illegally into the future, they were not schooled in the wisdom of God—they were the Babylonian prophets. In this instant they could not interpret because this Kairos [*the right time, critical, or opportune moment*] was fixed to a source. When Babylon failed—Daniel was switched on. King Nebuchadnezzar then consulted Daniel.

Daniel Stepped Outside of His Own Natural Wisdom and Experience.

HEAD OF GOLD

This head of gold represented the nation of Babylon, which is the engine room of the ungodly systems of the earth, which is still operational today.

Verse 44
In the days of those kings the God of heaven will set up a kingdom which will never be destroyed, and that kingdom will not be left for

another people; it will crush and put an end to all these kingdoms, but it will itself endure forever. NASB

Very important statement "**God of Heaven will set up the Kingdom**". **Set up**—comes from the Hebrew word **quwm**, which means: to be securely positioned and divinely arranged. We cannot subscribe to the Kingdom and still live lawlessly. As Kingdom citizens we must submit to laws. **Kingdom emphasis is about internal grandeur and not external appeal** like the systems of the world.

Worldly systems can be described as a system that is anti-Christ in nature that seeks to imprison our souls and define our lives in opposition to divine standards. These systems will mock anything that does not conform to its code. The world is advanced and propelled by the flesh.

Verse 43

And in that you saw the iron mixed with common clay, they will combine with one another in the seed of men; but they will not adhere to one another, even as iron does not combine with pottery. NASB

IN THE SEED OF MEN

This statement reveals that this image works in the lives of mankind and as we all know mankind is the primary communicator of the dynamics of the world. So logically if mankind is controlled by this false view, then the Kingdom of God would suffer. But alas we all know that that would not occur!

Unregenerate mankind will constantly seek to magnify external appeal, but they ignore internal substance. As we define the worldly character we must not only look "outside" the Church but inside as well.

Luke 3:10-14 states,

So the people asked him, saying, "What shall we do then?" He answered and said to them, "He who has two tunics, let him give to him who has none; and he who has food, let him do likewise." Then tax collectors also came to be baptized, and said to him, "Teacher, what shall we do?" And he said to them, "Collect no more than what is appointed for you." Likewise the soldiers asked him, saying, "And what shall we do?" So he said to them, "Do not intimidate anyone or accuse falsely, and be content with your wages."

- We see John the Baptist's Message... *Repent for the Kingdom of God is at hand...* People did not understand repentance—he had answers according to the groups he talked to.
- 1st group—give away—attacking selfishness—people coming to a place of seeing how they can help their brother.
- 2nd group—he says do not be corrupt and seduced—"love of money root of evil"—telling them to work in integrity—this attacks a Babylonian system of being competitive—we are always told to be the best—being better than our brother. John was saying that we must no longer be this way.
- 3rd group—soldiers. In the midst of the greatest military strength he is saying they must use their strength with control—do not take advantage of the people. Resonance—if we want same quality from people then we must accurately represent God. What we present is what is going to come back. When we model true love and community, masses will migrate after us—if we continue to demonstrate low levels, no one will come - we are called to go up.

EPHESUS
Paul taught and reasoned daily—results economic revolt. Reasoning and persuading—if we create a company of people that can have Kingdom ethics when dealing with buying and selling and how they spend their money we will definitely attack their society.

MARTIN LUTHER
Caused wars between nations in Europe for 200 years.

TWO ASPECTS OF CHRIST'S REFORMATION—MATTHEW 5:21-28
[Under the law there was external regulation to internal regulation therefore He kept saying that you heard but I am telling you] The flesh desires all sorts, but we must be internally regulated—the internal must take priority. Everything the Kingdom brings first has the ability to change us and then it has the ability to change society. Christ is calling us to build a society—the Bible opens up in a new way and we are seeing what God

actually wants. We begin to see what went wrong and how we became so Churchy. God is invalidating the traditional Church structures which is like a box—it captures and holds in bondage. God is not interested in so called Church structures He is interest in the Kingdom expressing itself through the Church.[5]

There were four major Empires spoken about:

- **Babylon** as the head of gold.
- **The Persians** as the chest and arms of silver conquered Babylon [Daniel 5:22-31].
- **The Greeks** as the belly and thighs of bronze conquered Persia [History teaches us that it was Alexander the Great].
- **The Roman Empire** conquered the Grecian empire as the legs of iron.

Unlike the empires that preceded it, when Rome invaded and conquered a country it would set up its own administration with its own governor appointed by the emperor of Rome but left the indigenous people in the land.

This is what was known as colonization. Rome governed its conquered territory through appointed governors who ruled with the authority of the emperor himself. The job of a Roman emperor was to govern his province in such a way as to make it a reflection of Rome.

A very interesting way that the Romans would take a territory was this—the Senate would meet and choose some businessmen to go into the territory about 2-3 years before the invasion and set up commerce and befriend the people. When that was accomplished then Rome would send in her armies and those businessmen would breach the city internally.

The model was now here for the King of the Kingdom of God to arrive.

- **The Forerunner is born**—John the Baptist and his assignment was to announce the arrival of the Kingdom—Matthew 3:2 *and saying, "Repent, for the kingdom of heaven is at hand!"*

---

[5] End of section from Author's book.

Now get this from the moment Jesus arrived on the scene as the God/man He was announced as "king" and not as "a priest"—Matthew 2:1-2, Luke 1:31-33, Luke 4:43

Now after Jesus was born in Bethlehem of Judea in the days of Herod the king, behold, wise men from the East came to Jerusalem, saying, "Where is He who has been born King of the Jews? For we have seen His star in the East and have come to worship Him."

And behold, you will conceive in your womb and bring forth a Son, and shall call His name Jesus. He will be great, and will be called the Son of the Highest; and the Lord God will give Him the throne of His father David. And He will reign over the house of Jacob forever, and of His kingdom there will be no end.

but He said to them, "I must preach the kingdom of God to the other cities also, because for this purpose I have been sent."

• This thing caused fear to take a hold of many—Matthew 2:3

When Herod the king heard this, he was troubled, and all Jerusalem with him.

• Even in His death the issue was over His Royal authority—John 18:33-38, John 19:12-13

Then Pilate entered the Praetorium again, called Jesus, and said to Him, "Are You the King of the Jews?" Jesus answered him, "Are you speaking for yourself about this, or did others tell you this concerning Me?" Pilate answered, "Am I a Jew? Your own nation and the chief priests have delivered You to me. What have You done?" Jesus answered, "My kingdom is not of this world. If My kingdom were of this world, My servants would fight, so that I should not be delivered to the Jews; but now My kingdom is not from here." Pilate therefore said to Him, "Are You a king then?" Jesus answered, "You say rightly that I am a king. For this cause I was born, and for this cause I have come into the world, that I should bear witness to the truth. Everyone who is of the truth hears My voice." Pilate said to Him, "What is truth?" And when he had said this, he went out again to the Jews, and said to them, "I find no fault in Him at all".

From then on Pilate sought to release Him, but the Jews cried out, saying, "If you let this Man go, you are not Caesar's friend. Whoever makes himself a king speaks against Caesar." When Pilate therefore heard that saying, he brought Jesus out and sat down in the judgment seat in a place that is called The Pavement, but in Hebrew, Gabbatha.

As soon as Jesus was baptized and started His earthly ministry, He preached the Kingdom of God—Matthew 4:17, Mark 1:14-15, Luke 4:43-44, John 3:3-5.

From that time Jesus began to preach and to say, "Repent, for the kingdom of heaven is at hand."

Now after John was put in prison, Jesus came to Galilee, preaching the gospel of the kingdom of God, and saying, "The time is fulfilled, and the kingdom of God is at hand. Repent, and believe in the gospel."

but He said to them, "I must preach the kingdom of God to the other cities also, because for this purpose I have been sent." And He was preaching in the synagogues of Galilee.

Jesus answered and said to him, "Most assuredly, I say to you, unless one is born again, he cannot see the kingdom of God." Nicodemus said to Him, "How can a man be born when he is old? Can he enter a second time into his mother's womb and be born?" Jesus answered, "Most assuredly, I say to you, unless one is born of water and the Spirit, he cannot enter the kingdom of God.

HERE ARE SOME OTHER SCRIPTURES—NIV

Matthew 10:7; Matthew 12:28; Matthew 18:23; Matthew 24:14; Luke 8:1; Luke 9:11; Luke 12:31; Luke 16:16-17; Luke 18:17; Luke 22:29

So it is very clear to see this—not only did Jesus rarely speak about being 'born again' neither did He make any of the other 'popular' themes the focus of His preaching. He had one message and that was 'The Kingdom'. Even when Nicodemus came to Him to ask about being 'born again' Jesus spoke to him about Kingdom!

- However, for the past 2000 years the true concept of kingdom has been lost, especially since the advent o f modern governments built on new concepts of governing, for example—democracy, socialism, communism and dictatorships.
- Even religion has caused a diversion from the message of the Kingdom of God into a moral system of belief. Causing religion to become an end in itself, distinguishing itself from the Kingdom concept with pride.
- In fact many religions take pride in separating "Church and State" and see the two as opposing entities with no common relationship.

Remember this, when we got saved and was born again, we were first born into the Kingdom of God and then assigned to a local church to be trained in order for us to reign and be useful in the Kingdom of God. This is very important, and I believe that once we understand this all the fighting between local churches would come to an end.

God then made some very significant changes to the Old Covenant System as the Temple where He formerly resided was completely destroyed. He divorced His Old covenant wife [Israel] and brought the promised judgement upon her and the system that she constantly violated. And now He established the New Covenant and introduced what no one had any idea concerning, The Church. I love what the following Scripture says concerning this:

Ephesians 3:2-6
if indeed you have heard of the dispensation of the grace of God which was given to me for you, how that by revelation He made known to me the mystery [as I have briefly written already, by which, when you read, you may understand my knowledge in the mystery of Christ], which in other ages was not made known to the sons of men, as it has now been revealed by the Spirit to His holy apostles and prophets: that the Gentiles should be fellow heirs, of the same body, and partakers of His promise in Christ through the gospel,

Colossians 1:25-27
of which I became a minister according to the stewardship from God which was given to me for you, to fulfill the word of God, the mystery which has been hidden from ages and from generations, but now has been revealed to His saints. To them God willed to make known what are the riches of the glory of this mystery among the Gentiles: which is Christ in you, the hope of glory.

We today are functioning under the New Covenant Age that is seeing the Kingdom of God being advanced throughout the earth. It is founded upon better promises than that of the Old Covenant System.

The Church in which we function is made up of both Jews and Gentiles. God fulfilled His promise that it was going to be the Jew first. As a matter of fact when the Church was revealed and launched in the Book of Acts the first members were all Jewish on that faithful Day of Pentecost. God fulfilled His promise then.

Next, we saw the salvation of the Gentiles and the Church was now in full swing.

Let us just revisit the launch of the New Covenant Church:

Acts 2:1-39
When the Day of Pentecost had fully come, they were all with one accord in one place. And suddenly there came a sound from heaven, as of a rushing mighty wind, and it filled the whole house where they were sitting. Then there appeared to them divided tongues, as of fire, and one sat upon each of them. And they were all filled with the Holy Spirit and began to speak with other tongues, as the Spirit gave them utterance. And there were dwelling in Jerusalem Jews, devout men, from every nation under heaven. And when this sound occurred, the multitude came together, and were confused, because everyone heard them speak in his own language. Then they were all amazed and marveled, saying to one another, "Look, are not all these who speak Galileans? And how is it that we hear, each in our own language in which we were born? Parthians and Medes and Elamites, those dwelling in Mesopotamia, Judea and Cappadocia, Pontus and Asia, Phrygia and Pamphylia, Egypt and the parts of Libya adjoining Cyrene, visitors from Rome, both Jews and

proselytes, Cretans and Arabs—we hear them speaking in our own tongues the wonderful works of God." So they were all amazed and perplexed, saying to one another, "Whatever could this mean?" Others mocking said, "They are full of new wine." But Peter, standing up with the eleven, raised his voice and said to them, "Men of Judea and all who dwell in Jerusalem, let this be known to you, and heed my words. For these are not drunk, as you suppose, since it is only the third hour of the day. But this is what was spoken by the prophet Joel: 'And it shall come to pass in the last days, says God, That I will pour out of My Spirit on all flesh; Your sons and your daughters shall prophesy, Your young men shall see visions, Your old men shall dream dreams. And on My menservants and on My maidservants I will pour out My Spirit in those days; And they shall prophesy. I will show wonders in heaven above And signs in the earth beneath: Blood and fire and vapor of smoke. The sun shall be turned into darkness, And the moon into blood, Before the coming of the great and awesome day of the LORD. And it shall come to pass That whoever calls on the name of the LORD Shall be saved.' "Men of Israel, hear these words: Jesus of Nazareth, a Man attested by God to you by miracles, wonders, and signs which God did through Him in your midst, as you yourselves also know—Him, being delivered by the determined purpose and foreknowledge of God, you have taken by lawless hands, have crucified, and put to death; whom God raised up, having loosed the pains of death, because it was not possible that He should be held by it. For David says concerning Him: 'I foresaw the LORD always before my face, For He is at my right hand, that I may not be shaken. Therefore my heart rejoiced, and my tongue was glad; Moreover my flesh also will rest in hope. For You will not leave my soul in Hades, Nor will You allow Your Holy One to see corruption. You have made known to me the ways of life; You will make me full of joy in Your presence.' "Men and brethren, let me speak freely to you of the patriarch David, that he is both dead and buried, and his tomb is with us to this day. Therefore, being a prophet, and knowing that God had sworn with an oath to him that of the fruit of his body, according to the flesh, He would raise up the Christ to sit on his throne, he, foreseeing this, spoke concerning the resurrection of the Christ, that His soul was not left in Hades, nor did His flesh see corruption. This Jesus God has raised up, of which we are all witnesses. Therefore being exalted to the right hand of God, and having received from the Father the promise of the Holy Spirit, He poured out this which you now see and hear. "For David did not ascend into the heavens, but he says himself: 'The LORD said to my Lord, "Sit at My right hand, Till I make Your enemies Your footstool."' "Therefore let all the house of Israel know assuredly that God has made this Jesus, whom you crucified, both Lord and Christ." Now when they heard this, they were cut to the heart, and said to Peter and the rest of the apostles, "Men and brethren, what shall we do?" Then Peter said to them, "Repent, and let every one of you be baptized in the name of Jesus Christ for the remission of sins; and you shall receive the gift of the Holy Spirit. For the promise is to you and to your children, and to all who are afar off, as many as the Lord our God will call."

Romans 1:16 Apostle Paul revealed:
For I am not ashamed of the gospel of Christ, for it is the power of God to salvation for everyone who believes, for the Jew first and also for the Greek.

The New Covenant was born through the sacrifice of Jesus' Life and the destruction of the Old Covenant Temple. And the New Covenant is an Eternal, Everlasting Covenant. There is no other covenant to come, and the Old Covenant System WILL NOT be revived. We are now living and would continue to live in this New Covenant, Kingdom Age. So we could be rest assured and continue to advance God's Kingdom in the earth.

Here is what the Scriptures say: Even under the Old Covenant System the promise of a New Covenant, which would be Everlasting was declared.

Jeremiah 31:31-34
"Behold, the days are coming, says the LORD, when I will make a new covenant with the house of Israel and with the house of Judah—not according to the covenant that I made with their fathers in the day that I took them by the hand to lead them out of the land of Egypt, My covenant which they broke, though I was a husband to

them, says the LORD. *But this is the covenant that I will make with the house of Israel after those days, says the* LORD: *I will put My law in their minds, and write it on their hearts; and I will be their God, and they shall be My people. No more shall every man teach his neighbor, and every man his brother, saying, 'Know the* LORD,' *for they all shall know Me, from the least of them to the greatest of them, says the* LORD. *For I will forgive their iniquity, and their sin I will remember no more."*

Hebrews 8:4-13

For if He were on earth, He would not be a priest, since there are priests who offer the gifts according to the law; who serve the copy and shadow of the heavenly things, as Moses was divinely instructed when he was about to make the tabernacle. For He said, "See that you make all things according to the pattern shown you on the mountain." But now He has obtained a more excellent ministry, inasmuch as He is also Mediator of a better covenant, which was established on better promises. For if that first covenant had been faultless, then no place would have been sought for a second. Because finding fault with them, He says: "Behold, the days are coming, says the LORD, *when I will make a new covenant with the house of Israel and with the house of Judah—not according to the covenant that I made with their fathers in the day when I took them by the hand to lead them out of the land of Egypt; because they did not continue in My covenant, and I disregarded them, says the* LORD. *For this is the covenant that I will make with the house of Israel after those days, says the* LORD: *I will put My laws in their mind and write them on their hearts; and I will be their God, and they shall be My people. None of them shall teach his neighbor, and none his brother, saying, 'Know the* LORD,' *for all shall know Me, from the least of them to the greatest of them. For I will be merciful to their unrighteousness, and their sins and their lawless deeds I will remember no more." In that He says, "A new covenant," He has made the first obsolete. Now what is becoming obsolete and growing old is ready to vanish away.*

Hebrews 12:18-24

For you have not come to the mountain that may be touched and that burned with fire, and to blackness and darkness and tempest, and the sound of a trumpet and the voice of words, so that those who heard it begged that the word should not be spoken to them anymore. [For they could not endure what was commanded: "And if so much as a beast touches the mountain, it shall be stoned or shot with an arrow." And so terrifying was the sight that Moses said, "I am exceedingly afraid and trembling."] But you have come to Mount Zion and to the city of the living God, the heavenly Jerusalem, to an innumerable company of angels, to the general assembly and church of the firstborn who are registered in heaven, to God the Judge of all, to the spirits of just men made perfect, to Jesus the Mediator of the new covenant, and to the blood of sprinkling that speaks better things than that of Abel.

This brings us to the end of this book, and it is my earnest prayer that you would have received much out of it. Stay Blessed—Author!

Let's check our understanding of the chapter "The Kingdom of God and the New Covenant."

1. How did the Chaldeans describe to the king, the only source who could tell what his dream was?

2. On what basis does the author liken the great statue to the worldly system that seeks entry into the Church?

3. How will we as individuals be able to identify between these 2 systems?

4. How will you explain "Not Cut out by Human Hands and Struck the Statue"? What is meant by this phrase?

5. Why is it not possible that the Kingdom is just contained within the Church? Explain with Scripture references.

6. In Jeremiah 31:38-40 speaks of two regions that are of utmost importance for us to understand. What are they? Why?

7. How does the above understanding apply to us today?

8. Why is it that the priests need to be multifaceted in the Kingdom of God? Explain with Scriptural backing.

9. What is meant by "they will combine but not adhere"?

10. Do you agree that the Kingdom of God entered the earth at the time period Daniel was talking about and is growing?

11. The author claims that "worldly systems can be described as anti-Christ in nature" do you agree? Explain.

12. Do you believe the Church possesses this worldly character within it and therefore requires scrutiny?

13. What were the 3 main Babylonian systems that John the Baptist wanted the early Believers to stand guard against? [Luke 3:10-14]

14. What are the 2 aspects of Christ's Reformation? [Matthew 5:21-28]

15. How was the Roman Empire different than its predecessors in terms of its administrative structure?

16. What was the method adopted by Rome in acquiring new territory?

17. How do you parallel this method with that of how God chose to establish His Kingdom in the earth?

18. What does Ephesians 3:2-6 & Colossians 1:25-27 reveal to us about the Church?

19. When and how did the launch of the New Covenant Church take place?

20. Which Scriptures assure us of the Everlasting feature of the New Covenant?

OTHER EXCITING TITLES
BY MICHAEL SCANTLEBURY

UNDERSTANDING THE DUAL ASPECTS OF FAITH

From the onset, Apostle Scantlebury presents the tenets of his tome, by eloquently contrasting the two dimensions of Faith: (1) where we use our Faith to acquire and believe God for new things and victories in Him and (2) where we use that same Faith to resist and battle against all odds that is thrown at us.

After defining the elements of faith, Apostle Michael empowers us with the tools to increase our faith: Our knowledge of God and the application of what we know. It's not enough to know what the Word of God says. What produces real faith is displayed when our actions match our belief.

Apostle Scantlebury gives us an accurate understanding of the benefits of our trials. Contrary to our Westernized belief, Faith and trials are mutually inclusive. We are encouraged to keep trusting God despite the opposition. Trusting God then becomes the substratum of having a pleasant relationship with Him.

UNDERSTANDING THE REVELATION

As we embark on this study, there are certain things that we need to first establish. Here are five things that I believe the book of Revelation is about:

1. Revelation is the most Biblical book in the Bible.
2. Revelation has a system of symbolism.
3. Revelation is a prophecy about imminent events – events that were about to break loose on the world of the First Century.
4. Revelation is a worship service.
5. Revelation is a book about dominion.

Also, we have to study The Revelation as a part of the entirety of Scripture and not as a separate book on its own. It ties in beautifully with the rest of the Bible and Israel's journey. So, as we study the prophecy within this book, we will see how it ties in with Jesus' prophecy recorded in Matthew 24 and many of the words spoken directly to the tribes of Israel. It was a powerful and very relevant book for the First Century Church and gives us today a clear picture of God's way of dealing with His people. When approached from this point of view, fresh realms of understanding will herald some fresh and powerful truths for us today.

Also, we need to bear in mind that the Bible is a record of Two Covenants; the Old Covenant which had a shelf life and was destined to come to an end. And then we have the New Covenant which is eternal and as such will never end. It has been eternally established by our King and Lord, Jesus the Christ. We need to add to this the understanding that the entire cannon of Scripture was written prior to AD 70.

ARE WE LIVING IN THE END TIMES OR THE LAST DAYS?

Whenever we hear this term "end-times or last-days" it conjures up all kinds of images in our minds: from the universe blowing up with the largest flames you could ever imagine! And that it would usher in a new heaven and a new earth. We also have presupposed in the body of Christ that before all of this would indeed occur, the righteous would be raptured away and then the world would be left a massive fire of destruction.

When you hear Christians mention the 'last days,' many just assume it's referring to the end of time and of the world. But the attentive Bible student asks, 'last days of what?' It seems obvious to me that the text is referring to the end of the Old Covenant-Temple aeon/age. When you read the New Testament through these lenses, all I can say is WOW! It makes a significant difference, when you read the Scriptures with the realization that the Bible was written FOR you and not TO you.

We need to also understand that "time of the end" and "end of time" are not one and the same thing. The Bible teaches about the "time of the end" but there is nothing taught about an "end of time."

FATHERS AND SONS – AN UNVEILING

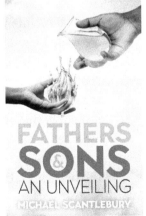

As we embark upon this study, there is something that I would like for us to first understand, and it is this: God the Father is the ultimate Father. There has never been anyone like Him, nor is there currently anyone like Him, nor will there ever be anyone like Him. He is in a class all by Himself.

Another thing that we need to understand moving forward is this: Respect produced by force and domination is not respect but fear.

Also, when we speak of sons, we are not only referring to the male gender, but we are speaking of **a new class in God**. Those that have been washed by the Blood of Jesus and have entered the

New Covenant with Him. Notice that in the Scriptures, it never states "Sons and Daughters of God."

John 1:12 states

But as many as received him, he gave them power to be made the sons of God, to them that believe in his name. ...

As such, I do believe that women can also be Apostles and in a broader scope, they qualify to "father" should that mantle be upon them.

HEAVEN & EARTH A BIBLICAL UNDERSTANDING

Whenever we today in this 21st Century read about heaven and earth in the Scriptures we need to be careful as to exactly what is being referred to. And here are some reasons as to why this must be.

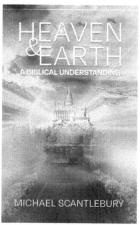

1. The original Bible was not written in our modern English, which is a far different language than Hebrew and Greek the original languages of the Holy Scriptures. Hence the reason for us to become avid students of the Word of God.
2. We, living today are not the original recipients of Scripture and as such we need to understand what the original recipients understood when they first received that Word.
3. We must be willing to let the Bible interpret itself and not hang on to our theories for the Scriptures.
4. That the Bible speaks of at least four Heavens and three earths. And as such we need to dig deep into the Word of God and find them and apply this understanding in our study.

Remember what the Scriptures say in Proverbs 25:2 *It is the glory of God to conceal the word, and the glory of kings to search out the speech.*

With that said let us now take a deeper dive and journey into the Word of God with the intention of extracting much needed revelation concerning these Heavens and Earths.

MY PONDERINGS

In this book before you the author has been engaged in pondering several subjects and as such, decided to put his thoughts in a book. As you read through these pages may the Lord use his thoughts to both inspire and bless you. Here are some of the subjects he has been pondering, with each one making up a chapter of this book:

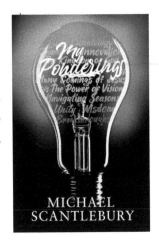

My Ponderings on The Kingdom of God

My Ponderings on The Church

My Ponderings on Innovation

My Ponderings on Wisdom and The Power of Vision

My Ponderings on Navigating Seasons

My Ponderings on Breakthroughs

My Ponderings on Unity

My Ponderings on The Many Comings of Jesus

My Ponderings on Eschatology

My Ponderings on Jesus the First Fruit of the Dead

My Ponderings on Understanding the Times

My Ponderings on Understanding the New Covenant

My Ponderings on Gold

UNDERSTANDING THE KINGDOM OF GOD AND THE CHURCH OF JESUS CHRIST

"This book is a game changer and will teach you what it means to be part of This Kingdom."

Pastor Marilyn Bailey
—Teleios Church, Johannesburg,
South Africa

"There is perhaps no greater time to revisit the spiritual and practical understanding of the kingdom of God than right now.

Apostle Scantlebury addresses and corrects, common misconceptions, explains the contrasts in the Kingdom of God and the kingdom of darkness, properly aligns the Kingdom and the Church, and propels us toward a holistic understanding of Kingdom life in the earth.

With great patience and clear articulation, Apostle Scantlebury lays out a compelling case for the people of God to give priority to understanding and walking in the principles of the Kingdom of God in life and ministry.

Do yourself a favour; set aside some time to read through and study this transformative volume. You will be challenged, changed, and equipped to be a proper representative of the kingdom of God."

Apostle Eric L. Warren—Eric Warren Ministries
Charlotte, North Carolina, USA

ESCHATOLOGY – A BIBLICAL VIEW

If you were a time traveler and traveled back to the time of say Abraham Lincoln and told him you were from the future in 21st century. What if he asked you how people communicated in the 21st century, and now you had to try and explain say how an email works. How would you explain it?

Would you use something he would be familiar with to describe it? Perhaps you would tell him that in the future postmen would ride horses at 500 mile per hour. Or you might tell him you could deliver a message by train from New York to LA in less than one day. You're trying to find a way to communicate how "fast" an email really is. But you're trying to do in a way that wouldn't totally blow his mind.

That's kind of the conundrum we have when trying to understand difficult verses in the Bible, especially in themes like eschatology. The prophetic writers of Scripture had to convey God's mysteries in language that their readers would understand.

Fast forward now 2-3,000 years later, and we are reading these prophetic Scriptures through a 21st century lens, and sometimes coming up with all kinds of weird speculative interpretations because we didn't understand what those Scriptures would have meant to a first century Believer, or a Jew living in the time of the OT Prophets.

The book before you plan to delve deeper into this and much more as it seeks to present you with a sensible view of eschatology.

THE RESTORATION OF ZION

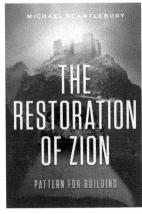

When you hear the word Zion, what comes to mind? As Christians, we've sung the choruses and the hymns about Zion or Mount Zion, but do we fully understand just what we're singing about? Do we know what it is? The Bible promises the full restoration of Zion, and if we don't fully know what Zion is, what then do we anticipate in terms of its restoration?

The greatest hindrance to accurate interpretation and application of Scripture is a futuristic view of Scripture. This futuristic view continues to rob the Believer of experiencing God in His fullness in the here and now.

In this book, we will uncover within the Scriptures exactly what Zion actually represents to the New Testament Believer. So lay down any preconceived ideas you may have, delve into the pages of this book, and let it speak truth to you.

AS IT WAS IN THE BEGINNING SO SHALL IT BE...

Have you ever wondered about life and all of its intricacies? Why are we here on planet earth? What is out there in deep dark space? Who created it all in its majesty and wonder with the brilliancy of everything that surrounds us?

Since time began, man has tried to explain things regarding the known world. One forward thinker put forth a theory that the world was flat. That was refuted by more research. Study and research and pondering some more have revealed some truth about our world but not all the questions are yet answered.

While many of us as Christians enjoy documentaries on the pondering of the many ways we may have "gotten here" beginning with the theory of alien transports dropping us off, to the idea of a cosmic slime pit which one day came to life, so truly the only authority we have as born-again followers of Jesus Christ is the book of Genesis, the very first book of the Holy Scriptures, which simply states: "In the beginning God created the heavens and the earth." Genesis 1:1

We will broach the answers to these and other questions only God's inspired word, the Holy Bible will answer the many questions at hand.

We will begin our journey into the heart and mind of this incredible Creator to learn the reason and purpose for our existence. And as we take that incredible journey, we would seek to come to terms with the revealed, eventual outcome of our existence and life upon planet earth.

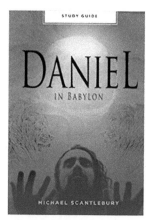

STUDY GUIDE – DANIEL IN BABYLON

This is an exciting study into the present truth lifestyle illustrated through the lives of Daniel and his friends. Whether you'll be meeting with others in a group or going through this book on your own, you've made an excellent decision by choosing to read **DANIEL in Babylon** and studying it in-depth with this guide.

This is a seminal study with strong Apostolic messaging, yet its flowing style allows for easy assimilation of biblical truths, and provides accurate insights for the cerebral Believer, who like Daniel and his companions, are usually the target of the world system. In this book various methodologies are outlined through which, spiritual Babylon seeks to entice the brightest and best of every Godly generation, to acculturize, rob of spiritual identity and manipulate to promote world kingdom end.

PRINCIPLES FOR VICTORIOUS LIVING: VOL II

The initial purpose of the five-fold ministry is for the perfecting or maturing of the Saints, which leads to its next intention, which is the real work of the ministry of Jesus Christ, reconciling the world back to the Father. This book lends itself to help in the maturing of the Saints. It adds insight and strategies that help in achieving exponential personal growth preparing one for the real work of the ministry. This is a volume of information and revelation needed in such a time 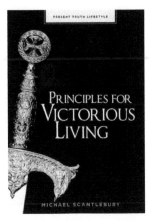 as this, when maturity and focus are the needed key components that bring us an overcoming victory in this realm and advance the Kingdom of God.

PRINCIPLES FOR VICTORIOUS LIVING: VOL I

The information contained herein is well balanced with a spiritual maturity that keenly stems from wisdom and revelation in the knowledge of Christ. This is the anointing of an Apostle, and the truths that our brother shares will certainly cause you to excel in the Kingdom of God long before this life is over when later we enter the eternals. There's so much to experience today in this life, and Michael extracts so much from the Word of God to facilitate that. His insight of 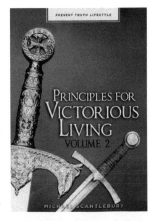 revelation and ability to interpret and articulate what his spirit receives from the Lord are powerful.

PRESENT TRUTH LIFESTYLE - DANIEL IN BABYLON

This is a seminal study with strong Apostolic messaging, yet its flowing style allows for easy assimilation of biblical truths, and provides accurate insights for the cerebral Believer, who like Daniel and his companions, are usually the target of the world system. In this book various methodologies are outlined through which, spiritual Babylon seeks to entice the brightest and best of every Godly generation, to acculturize, rob of spiritual identity and manipulate to promote world kingdom end.

But thanks be to God, there is still a generation in the earth spiritually alert enough to operate within the world system, yet deploy their talents and giftings to bring honour and glory to God. Those with the Daniel mindset will decode dreams and visions and interpret judgements written on the kingdoms of this world in this season.

ESTHER PRESENT TRUTH CHURCH

In a season where the Church co-exists harmoniously with truth and error, this book provides us with a precision tool and well-calibrated instrument of change that is able to fine-tune the global Body of Christ.

The Book of Esther is rich with revelation that is still valid and applicable for the day in which we live. Hidden within its pages is a powerful "present truth" message. The lives of the people involved and the conditions that are seen have spiritual parallels for the Church. Our destiny as the Body of Christ is revealed. The preparations and conditions we must attain to are all similar.

THE FORTRESS CHURCH

According to Webster's English Dictionary "fortress" is defined as: a fortified place: stronghold, *especially*: A large and permanent fortification sometimes including a town. A place that is protected against attack. This book seeks to describe what is a "Fortress Church". We would be looking into the dynamics of this Church as described in Jacob's vision in Genesis Chapter 28, 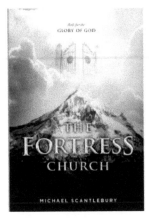 also as described by the Prophet Isaiah, in Isaiah Chapter 2 and as the one detailed in a Psalm of the sons of Korah in Psalms Chapter 48. We would also be looking at a working model of this type of church as found at Antioch in the Book of Acts. Finally we would be exploring The Church at Ephesus, where the Apostle Paul by the Holy Spirit revealed some powerful descriptions of The Church.

CALLED TO BE AN APOSTLE

This autobiography spans fifty-two years of my life on the earth thus far and I have the hope of living several more... Our home was always packed with young people and we did enjoy times of really wonderful fellowship! Although we were experiencing these wonderful times of fellowship my appetite and desire to grow in the things of God  continued unabated. I continued to read anything and everything that I could put my hands on that would strengthen my life. I began reading Wigglesworth, Moody, Finney, Idahosa, Lake, and the list went on and on! But the more I read the more this question burned in my heart–"*why is it that every time we hear/read about a move of God, it is always miles away and in another country? Why can't I experience some of the things that I am reading about?*" Little did I know the Lord would answer that desire!

LEAVENED REVEALED

The Bible has a lot to say about *leaven* and its effects upon the Believer. Leaven as an ingredient gives a false sense of growth. In the New Testament there are at least six types of *leaven* spoken about and we will be exploring them in detail, in order to ensure that our lives are completely free of the first five, and completely influenced by the sixth! These types of leaven include the following: The leaven of the Pharisees; The leaven of the Sadducees; The leaven of the Galatians; The leaven of Herod; The leaven of the Corinthians. However, the Leaven of the Kingdom of God is the only type of leaven that has the power and capacity to bring about true growth and lasting change to our lives.

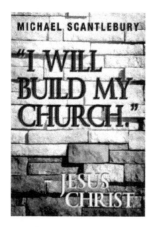

I WILL BUILD MY CHURCH — JESUS CHRIST

"For we are his *masterpiece*, created in Christ Jesus for good works that God prepared long ago to be our way of life." Ephesians 2:10

What a powerful picture of The Church of Jesus Christ–His Masterpiece! Reference to a *masterpiece* lends to the idea that there are other pieces and among them all, this particular one stands head and shoulders above the rest! This is so true when it comes to The Church that Jesus Christ is building; when you place it alongside everything else that God has created, The Church is by far His Masterpiece!

JESUS CHRIST THE APOSTLE AND HIGH PRIEST OF OUR PROFESSION

There is a dimension to the apostolic nature of Jesus Christ that I would like to capture in His one-on-one encounters with several people during the time He walked the face of the earth and functioned as Apostle. In this book we will explore several significant encounters that Jesus Christ had with different people where valuable principles and insight can be gleaned. They are designed to change your life.

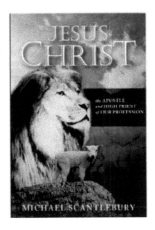

FIVE PILLARS OF THE APOSTOLIC

It has become very evident that a new day has dawned in the earth, as the Lord restores the foundational ministry of the Apostle back to His Church. This book will give you a clear and concise understanding of what the Holy Spirit is doing in The Church today.

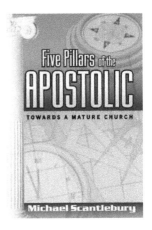

APOSTOLIC PURITY

In every dispensation, in every move of God's Holy Spirit to bring restoration and reformation to His Church, righteousness, holiness and purity has always been of utmost importance to the Lord. This book will challenge your to walk pure as you seek to fulfil God's Will for your life and ministry.

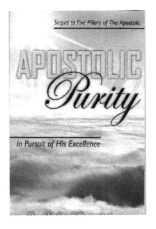

GOD'S NATURE EXPRESSED THROUGH HIS NAMES

How awesome it would be when we encounter God's Nature through the varied expressions of His Names. His Names give us reference and guidance as to how He works towards and in us as His people–and by extension to society! As a matter of fact it adds a whole new meaning to how you draw near to Him; and by this you can now begin to know His Ways because you have come into relationship with His Nature.

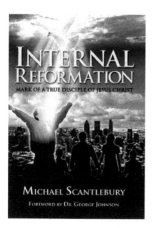

INTERNAL REFORMATION

Internal Reformation is multifaceted. It is an ecclesiology laying out the blue print of The Church Jesus Christ is building in today's world. At the same time it is a manual laying out the modus operandi of how Believers are called to function as dynamic, militant over-comers who are powerful because they carry internally the very character and DNA of Jesus Christ.

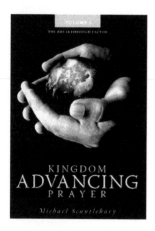

KINGDOM ADVANCING PRAYER VOL I

The Church of Jesus Christ is stronger and much more determined and equipped than she has ever been, and strong, aggressive, powerful, Spirit-Filled, Kingdom-centred prayers are be-ing lifted in every nation in the earth. This kind of prayer is released from the heart of Father God into the hearts of His people, as we seek for His Glory to cover the earth as the waters cover the sea.

APOSTOLIC REFORMATION

If the axe is dull, And one does not sharpen the edge, Then he must use more strength; But wisdom brings success." (Ecclesiastes 10:10) For centuries The Church of Jesus Christ has been using quite a bit of strength while working with a dull axe (sword, Word of God, revelation), in trying to get the job done. This has been largely due to the fact that she has been functioning without Apostles, the ones who have been graced and anointed by the Lord, with the ability to sharpen.

KINGDOM ADVANCING PRAYER VOL II

Prayer is calling for the Bridegroom's return, and for the Bride to be made ready. Prayers are storming the heavens and binding the "strong men" declaring and decreeing God's Kingdom rule in every jurisdiction. This is what we call Kingdom Advancing Prayer. What a *Glorious Day* to be *Alive* and to be in the *Will* and *Plan of Father God*! *Hallelujah*!

KINGDOM ADVANCING PRAYER VOLUME III

One of the keys to the amazing rise to greater functionality of The Church is the clear understanding of what we call Kingdom Advancing Prayer. This kind of prayer reaches into the very core of the demonic stronghold and destroys demonic kings and princes and establishes the Kingdom and Purpose of the Lord. This is the kind of prayer that Jesus Christ engaged in, to bring to pass the will of His Father while He was upon planet earth.

IDENTIFYING AND DEFEATING THE JEZEBEL SPIRIT

I declare to you with the greatest of conviction that we are living in the days when Malachi 4:5-6 is being fulfilled. Elijah in his day had to confront and deal with a false spiritual order and government that was established and set up by an evil woman called Jezebel and her spineless husband called Ahab. This spirit is still active in the earth and in The Church; however the Lord is restoring His holy Apostles and Prophets to identify and destroy this spirit as recorded in Revelation 2:18-23.

9 781486 625307